Lisa Aparicio, series editor

be

ENGAGING YOUTH IN EVANGELISM

Wesley Parry • Denise Holland
Daniel Latu • Christiano Malta
Wouter van der Zeijden • Dario Richards

CREDITS
Authors: Kenny Wade, Wesley Parry, Denise Holland, Daniel Latu, Christiano Malta, Wouter van der Zeijden, Dario Richards

Book and Series Editor: Lisa Aparicio

Copy Editors: Hailey Teeter, Emily Reyes, and Emily Knocke

Cover Design: Christian Cardona

TABLE OF CONTENTS

ABOUT THIS SERIES

"How do you guide youth to be confident in evangelism?"

"What should I be thinking about to make sure my youth are growing in their faith?"

"Sometimes I don't feel like I know what I'm doing as a leader. How am I going to help my youth develop their own leadership skills?"

We frequently hear questions like these from youth leaders all around the world. They are youth leaders in small churches and large churches. They are formally trained youth pastors and lay volunteer youth workers. Maybe you've asked questions like these as well.

This three-book series is our way of reaching out to local youth leaders to encourage and equip you in the deeply meaningful work you are doing. The challenge is that youth ministry is diverse, with ever-changing cultural nuances to navigate. Thus, we have chosen to focus each of these books on one of our core strategies in NYI — evangelism (BE), discipleship (DO), and leadership development (GO). These core strategies have served youth ministry in the Church of the Nazarene well since its earliest days. We have also invited in a diverse team of writers to help us share a balanced perspective with you. We trust you will enjoy this blend of voices and that the mix of perspectives will provide connection to your ministry setting no matter what your context.

Wherever you find yourself in ministry, know that you are appreciated, that you are prayed for, and that you bring more skills to youth ministry than you know.

May God bless you.

Gary Hartke
Director, Nazarene Youth International

PREFACE

When we talk about evangelism (BE), discipleship (DO), and leadership development (GO), it is generally easier for us to access voices similar to our own — ones who share ideas and strategies we are already familiar with. However, we believe that our three core strategies in Nazarene Youth International deserve a more nuanced discussion. We started this conversation in 2013 with a renewed emphasis on our core strategies and started talking about BE, DO, and GO.

Evangelism:
BE God's light, even in the dark places of our world.

Discipleship:
DO the hard work of becoming more like Jesus as you walk with others.

Leadership Development:
GO out into your community and learn as a servant leader.

As the conversation of BE, DO, and GO spread, we wanted to help the lessons emerging from those conversations to spread as well. We wanted the lessons to be taught by diverse voices, each bringing a unique perspective to the global conversation. To accomplish this, we needed a global team of writers and the result was this series, which we believe is a true expression of what it means to be a global church.

We trust that you will benefit greatly from these diverse authors. A brief introduction for each one is provided at the beginning of their chapter. As you read, you will be reminded of the diversity of our church, not only through the content, but even in little ways, such as spelling. We have made the intentional choice to keep the vocabulary and spelling style for each author consistent with what is used in their part of the world. When a chapter has been translated from a different language, the spelling and vocabulary are more reflective of the translator's home country.

May God bless you in your ministry as you seek to actively engage your youth in evangelism, discipleship, and leadership development. We believe these books are starting points to help you move forward in your ministry with more intentionality. Where will you go from here? We invite you to take your place in the global story of BE, DO, and GO.

Lisa Aparicio
Editor
Ministry Development Coordinator, Nazarene Youth International

ACKNOWLEDGMENTS

The formation of a global writing team required the input and support of many individuals. It began with an invitation for all of our regional youth coordinators to share names with us of youth leaders from their region who excelled in evangelism, discipleship, or leadership development. Without the support and discernment of Ronald Miller (Africa Region), Janary Suyat de Godoy (Asia-Pacific Region), Diego Lopez (Eurasia Region), Milton Gay (Mesoamerica Region), Jimmy De Gouveia (South America Region), and Justin Pickard (USA/Canada Region), these books wouldn't have happened.

Video conference calls were hosted with all of the 18 writers to share, collaborate, and ultimately shape the structure of these books. The calls were organized and led by Shannon Greene (Global NYI Office). Her overall contribution to this project was absolutely invaluable. Kenny Wade (Youth in Mission) also participated in each call to share the background of the BE, DO, GO initiative. The context he provided gave the whole project a solid foundation to build on. Kenny also contributed to the series as the author of the introductions.

Ultimately though, these books wouldn't have been possible without the hard work of each of our writers. They have shared from their hearts about how they see God at work through the church's efforts to engage youth in evangelism, discipleship, and leadership development.

Africa
Wesley Parry (Evangelism)
Nicholas Barasa (Discipleship)
Lesego Shibambo
(Leadership Development)

Asia-Pacific
Daniel Latu (Evangelism)
Bakhoh Jatmiko (Discipleship)
Cameron Batkin
(Leadership Development)

Eurasia
Wouter van der Zeijden (Evangelism)
Nabil Habiby (Discipleship)
Kat Wood (Leadership Development)

Mesoamerica
Dario Richards (Evangelism)
Milton Gay (Discipleship)
Odily Díaz (Leadership Development)

South America
Christiano Malta (Evangelism)
Jaime Román Araya (Discipleship)
Thiago Nieman Ambrósio
(Leadership Development)

USA/Canada
Denise Holland (Evangelism)
Andrea Sawtelle (Discipleship)
Phil Starr (Leadership Development)

INTRODUCTION

Kenny Wade

Kenny Wade serves as the Youth in Mission Coordinator. For Kenny, youth ministry helps us think creatively about what it means for God's kingdom to come here on earth as we minister alongside youth whose lives are committed to Christ. He believes that we are people of Good News who have placed our hope in the life-giving resurrection of Christ.

One of my earliest memories of evangelism is in northeastern South Africa. As an eight-year-old missionary kid, I remember watching my parents walking and talking with people in the local village. As they listened, they got to know the place, people, language, and culture. When the opportunity arose, they shared why they were there. A couple of Americans walking around in a tribal village in South Africa tends to evoke questions. As my parents answered these questions, they began to share the good news of Jesus.

> **My role as a follower of Christ was to be present, available, and cooperative with the Spirit of Jesus; not to play Holy Spirit junior. It wasn't my job to convict, judge, or save.**

Walking and talking (Matthew 4:18). It seems like Jesus did a lot of that. Walking everywhere with his friends. Talking with them about everyday and eternal things. Meeting new people. Sharing meals together. Discussing faith. Asking questions. Walking and talking seems to fill a majority of the in-between spaces in the four Gospels. Simply being in life together.

No other friendship has shaped my perspective of evangelism more than Bobby's. Bobby and I first met on the sidelines of our sons' football practice. In getting to know him, I attempted to intentionally embrace what John Wesley described as prevenient grace: God is already present and active in drawing people deeper into relationship with Him.[1] I tried to trust that God's presence was already moving in Bobby's life. My role as a follower of Christ was to be present, available, and cooperative with the Spirit of Jesus; not to play Holy Spirit junior. It wasn't my job to convict, judge, or save. With Bobby, I wanted to commit to the authentic and even more challenging long-term work of trusting God's already present and active Spirit — but this has not always been my approach.

My understanding of evangelism during my teen years was somewhat distorted. Somehow, sharing the good news of Jesus had become more about me trying to earn God's favor. Evangelism was not about being with God and others. It became more about telling enough people about Jesus so that I could be okay with God. Evangelism was about me getting people to follow Jesus rather than joining God in what He was already doing in their lives. It felt very forced. There was a prayer formula to follow, and if it was done and said right then a person was suddenly transformed into being a Christian. The last thing I wanted to do was somehow turn my new friendship with Bobby into a project about my own issues of self-esteem. I wanted to avoid commodifying our friendship and objectifying Bobby (or myself) at all costs. I had to ask myself if the only reason I was getting to know him was to share about Christ, or if I genuinely cared about him as a person regardless of his beliefs. There was probably a little bit of both of these in my intentions at the beginning of Bobby and I's friendship.

Evangelism is not something we *do* to other people, but a way of living life.

However, I have found that my efforts of evangelism can become more focused on the expected outcome of the person's decision rather than attentiveness to what Christ is already doing in his or her life. When I allow this outcome-motivation to be my relational posture, the person too easily becomes a project to complete rather than a person to be loved. My interior posture of evangelism can be a telling reflection of my personal sense of self-worth. This reflection leads me to ask myself, "Why am I evangelizing?"

While on a retreat as a young youth worker, my tension and frustration with evangelism surfaced. I was confronted with the idea that sharing Jesus was not about saying a certain prayer or getting teenagers to do what I wanted them to do for their own good. This was a hard idea for me to comprehend, but it transformed the way I saw evangelism. Evangelism is not something we *do* to other people, but a way of living life. A way to BE. Evangelism is about the good and hard work of being close with God and allowing God to work through me. To trust God with the results. To BE who God wants me to be every day. To BE with others. Evangelism is a way of paying attention to the Spirit of God already at work in the world through the lives of others and then joining Him. In the book *Being Real*, I share about the invitation to allow the image of God in me to call out to the image of God in another person.[2] This allows the Spirit of Christ to lead instead of my own muddled motivations and misguided techniques.

Remember my friend, Bobby? When we first met at football practice I resisted inflicting myself, my life, or my vocation as a youth pastor onto him. He knew what I did for a living. He shared with me that he had grown up being a part of a church but was not very interested or impressed with religion overall. This felt like a test for me. Could I be trusted with a friendship between the two of us? God had already initiated the work of his grace in both Bobby and myself. The question was, would I choose to be aware of that reality in the journey between us?

When Jesus met the woman at the well, he approached her with His need for a drink of water. Did you catch that? His need; not hers (John 4:7-14). The rich young ruler comes to Jesus with a question (Luke 18). Jesus responds with a statement that causes the man to ask even deeper questions about his life and faith. When Paul shares about the resurrection of Christ in Athens, he takes the time to get to know their city, culture, and context before speaking (Acts 17). Paul listens and learns. He quotes their poets to engage their imagination and invites them to consider Christ through the lens of their local faith. Our needs. Other's questions. Awareness of context. Our efforts of evangelism must be suited to our context and to the relationships of our cultural landscape. Methods effective in my setting may be out of place in yours, but if we are seeking a method of evangelism that assumes God is already at work in His mission of redeeming the world, then relationships will be a priority and creativity a necessity. Both Paul and Jesus modified their methods of evangelism to share the Good News with multiple strategies for individual people and groups of all sizes. We cannot have a relationship with everyone, but we can show respect towards everyone as being made in His image.

The most challenging relationships through which to share Good News are among those that know us best — our families, friends, neighbours, church, classmates, and co-workers. They know what we are really like and what it is truly like to BE with us. They know if we are just talking about Good News or truly living it: being Good News. Evangelism is coming to Jesus to BE. And then, it is allowing Jesus to shape us to BE in relationship with others.

In the stories from Scripture mentioned above, who were the ones in need? Evangelism can happen when we allow ourselves to be in need, and God can use those needs to share Good News with others. Maybe the small need of a tool to fix something at my house could be a relational bridge. I simply could buy the tool and fix the problem, or I could humbly ask a neighbor to lend theirs to me. This action of borrowing could lead to a bridge of relational Good News.

God's love, forgiveness, and hope in Christ can be expressed in life through the Spirit in a way of choosing to live with intentional need. Evangelism is not meant to be a burden we project on others. When we draw close to God, God draws close to us, and we can be who we truly are in Christ. God's Spirit is already at work in people's lives, wooing them (prevenient grace), and our invitation is to join Him and follow the Spirit's leading in the process.

As the sport season wrapped up and I realised I potentially wouldn't see Bobby for many months, I stopped by his house to exchange contact information. Standing at his front door, he asked me an abrupt question, "What time is your church?" This took me by surprise. I quickly responded, "You know this isn't about church or religion for me but relationship with Jesus, right?" Bobby said, "Yeah, that's why I like talking to you." Maybe there is something to this waiting on God stuff and joining Him in what He is already doing after all.

Can we agree to make a few assumptions together as we enter this adventure of exploring evangelism? Let's assume the good news of Jesus must first and foremost be something we embrace by choosing to personally BE with Jesus. Daily. Weekly. Always. Then we can assume the good news of Christ will flow from our lives unforced. Can we then assume that as God's Spirit is already present and working in our lives, He is also at work in the lives of others? Then let's agree to be approachable: the kind of people others like talking to about everyday life and the hope we have in faith through Christ. All the riff-raff of the town liked being with Jesus (Luke 15:1-2). He was the life of the party for the outcasts. Let's assume we are among them, and enjoy God's grace. Let's BE Good News.

CHAPTER 1

Biblical Foundations of Evangelism

Wesley Parry

Wesley Parry is an Impact Team Member who serves in Johannesburg, South Africa. Youth ministry is exciting to him because youth are ever-changing, always moving and very dynamic. He gets really excited when young people are involved in leadership roles in the church. Wesley loves seeing the desire of youth transition from receiving to serving.

As we start this journey and seek to more faithfully engage youth in evangelism, we want to explore the biblical foundations of evangelism. We will look at the ministry of Jesus and the early church in order to reflect on the diversity with which they shared the Good News and the consistency with which it flowed out of their interactions with people. However, to begin, let's remind ourselves of what our life-changing message is.

Our Message

Christ crucified and raised from the dead.

We must never forget that the message we are to bring to the world is a simple and amazing truth. It will never change. From the beginning until the New Jerusalem, the message must be Jesus incarnate, crucified, and raised from the dead. It proclaims the radical love of a God willing to take on human flesh and live among us. It embraces the scandalous truth of a God surrendering even to death on a cross in order to redeem His creation. It declares the hope-filled power of Christ raised from the dead. This message matters because it has transformative power in our lives — that radical love is available to us. Jesus' death is what brings us forgiveness and new life in Christ. The same power that raised Jesus from the dead is available to us to raise us back to life. This message matters. This message is what the world needs to hear.

We all have our own stories of surrender and transformation. If we think we don't, then we have not given enough thought to the work of God in our lives. Sometimes youth feel they don't have a story to share, and we need to help them recognize the ways we see God at work in their hearts and lives. In the end, however, our own stories are only testimonies to the truth of the message itself. As Paul says in 2 Corinthians 4:5, "We do not preach ourselves, but Jesus Christ as Lord, and ourselves as your servants for Jesus' sake." Any form of evangelism must point to Jesus. We must, as Paul declares, "Preach Christ crucified" at all times (1 Corinthians 1:23).

Go now and leave your life of sin.

In an encounter with an adulterous woman, Jesus conveys a very important message that modern evangelism sometimes seems to avoid. Before sending the woman on her way, Jesus says "go now and leave your life of sin" (John 8:11). When the evangelist and church planter Harmon Schmelzenbach arrived in Swaziland in the early 1900s, he did not know the language, but as he spent time there he learned the word for repent: "*phendugani.*" From his rock he could be seen preaching his message of phendugani.[1] Repentance is the unfortunate victim of modern evangelism, where we have the "quick, do you believe?" salvation and "sinners prayer" solutions; but nobody wants to talk about sin. Jesus, on the other hand, was always confronting sin (Matthew 21:12-17, Luke 17:1-4, Matthew 18:15-20). Jesus Himself said, "I came not to call the righteous, but sinners to repentance" (Mark 2:17). As biblical evangelists, our full message is not just God's love, but also His holiness, righteousness, and forgiveness of sin. This we must proclaim unapologetically.

Jesus the Evangelist

It is worthwhile to ask, how is it that Jesus proclaimed this message of repentance and was considered a friend of sinners, while the Church has proclaimed the same message and repelled those we have sought to bring to Christ? Jesus was relational and personal, valuing friendship over efforts. Every action and word Jesus said and did was weighed out and intentional. As such, I want to discuss some of the characteristics we see Jesus expressing in His everyday interactions with people. We would do well to embody, and help our youth embody, these characteristics as we witness to others if we wish to compel rather than repel them.

Assurance

We must know, without a doubt, that God has called each of us to take the gospel to the world. This calling is something we must understand and accept in the very depths of our heart, as Jesus did. This assurance allows us to be obedient to whatever task God has for us. Sometimes we may be called to just till the soil, other times we will be the one to plant the seed, and still other times God will give us the role of watering the seed. It is thrilling to be trusted with the opportunity of bringing in the harvest, but that is not always going to be our role. Assurance allows us to trust God with the results.

Intentional

Jesus was intentional with all of His encounters. Jesus met the woman at the well while He was on a journey, but He could have made the trip in a way that avoided Samaria. Instead, He intentionally takes a route into enemy territory so He can connect with people who need Him. As Nazarenes, we believe God's prevenient grace is intentionally drawing all people to Himself. Our intentionality manifests itself in how we obediently come alongside the work God is already doing in their lives in order to bring the word God has for them.

Perhaps we as evangelists should follow Jesus' example and stop talking during the entire encounter, beginning to ask questions and listen more.

Humility

This is, of course, a characteristic we would associate with Jesus. The Scriptures themselves spell this out for us. "Have the same mindset as Christ Jesus: who being in very nature God, did not consider equality with God something to be used to His own advantage; rather, He made Himself nothing by taking the very nature of a servant, being made in human likeness" (Philippians 2:5-7). This humility is central to authentic friendship and is key in breaking down barriers in people.

Willingness to Listen

A willingness to listen is imperative for one-on-one evangelism. Evangelism is more than proclaiming Jesus; it is also listening to the inmost desires, hopes, and hurts of the people of the world. This often means sacrificing our own desires in order to be present when God calls us. Jesus is often seen asking questions of people: "What are you discussing together?" (Luke 24:15), "What do you want me to do for you?" (Mark 10:51), "Who do you say that I am?" (Luke 9:20). In the Gospel of Matthew alone, Jesus asks 94 questions during evangelistic conversations.[2] Perhaps we as evangelists should follow Jesus' example and stop talking during the entire encounter, beginning to ask questions and listen more.

Joy

Throughout the Scriptures, we see Christ demonstrating a deep and abiding joy in the Father and in the coming of the Kingdom. This has been and remains the greatest form of evangelism that we Christians have — our testimonies and the resulting joy we have in the Lord (Acts 4:33).

Approaches to Evangelism

Jesus showed as much creativity in sharing the good news with those around Him as we see in creation itself. There is not a one-size-fits-all evangelistic method. However, there are some common approaches we see Jesus and the early church using which can give us some valuable insights into evangelism.

Personal Evangelism

When we teach Bible classes or when we hold evangelism campaigns and services, we are evangelizing and teaching. However, personal evangelism is what we see Jesus consistently doing throughout His ministry. It is what we see in John 4 with the Samaritan woman at the well. The story is a great example of one-on-one personal evangelism, and we should give attention to the process and steps Jesus goes through in this conversation.

1. The first thing Jesus does is make contact. This contact can be made anywhere with anyone. For some of you this looks like an outreach, but for others it looks like your coworker in the cubicle next to you, someone in your school, or even someone at the local shopping center. For Jesus, it was a woman He met at the well. Just as Jesus defied the social and religious norms to speak with her (she was a woman and she was a Samaritan), we must not allow any barriers to come between us and making this contact. Likewise, if we truly believe that the gospel is for all, then there should be no barriers we are not willing to cross to make contact with those whom God is prompting us toward. We need to help our youth become more attentive to these opportunities, and we need to model such attentiveness as well.

2. Jesus establishes a conversation with the woman. For some, this can take days, and for others it takes months, but once the conversation has been established, we must watch for the opportunity to shift the conversation to Jesus. However, we cannot begin with this. The "in-your-

face evangelism" that comes out swinging is not as effective anymore because it immediately makes people put up barriers. We even see Jesus avoiding this by first asking the woman for a drink of water. Only after the contact and conversation about water has been established does He transition the conversation by talking about living water. Shifting the conversation to Jesus is often intimidating for youth. We need to help them consider what those moments might look like and how they can be prepared and trust the Holy Spirit's guidance.

3. Jesus reveals that He is the Messiah. For us, the declaration is that Jesus is Lord of our life. We must be careful that our life is a faithful reflection of Christ so that our life matches our words. As a child, my mother would always tell me to "practice what I preach." As believers who want to reach the world for Jesus, we must embody what we are saying. We can help prepare our youth for these opportunities by helping them remember that our actions are our first witness — for or against the story of God.

4. We see the woman run back to the city and testify everything Jesus had said. The story isn't clear as to whether or not she fully believes at this point or if her faith comes later. Sometimes we have to be okay with the uncertainty of how someone receives our witness. It is important for our youth to understand that our work is to be faithful to share as God leads, but that it is the Holy Spirit who will convict and bring them to the point of decision.

5. Jesus uses the multiplication method to reach others in addition to the woman. The entire city, through the conversion of one woman, would hear the good news of the Messiah as a result of Jesus' ministry to her. Jesus was intentional with everything He did.

Another example of one-on-one personal evangelism is Jesus' interaction with the expert in the Law (Luke 10). This Jewish lawyer asks Jesus what he must do to have eternal life. Jesus affirms the expert's own answer, that one must love God and love ones' neighbor. How easy would evangelism be if people just walked up to us with this question? We could easily answer them and then lead them into prayer and salvation. Jesus, however, sees the heart of the lawyer and turns the question back on him. The lawyer accurately answers Jesus question and summarizes the Law: "You shall love the Lord your God will all your heart, and with all your soul and with all your strength and with all your mind, and your neighbor as yourself" (Luke

10:27). Jesus replies in verse 28, "do this and you will live." Easy, right? Well, in this case, no. Jesus discerns that the heart of the man was not sincere but was "putting Jesus to the test," as Luke writes (Luke 10:25). And the man responds with yet another question.

We will also encounter people like this today, people who are more interested in debating religious ideas rather than seeking after Christ. We should never hold this against them, giving them as much love and energy as anyone else we speak to. In this story, Jesus refuses to join in the theological debate (though I'm sure He would win); instead He answers the question with a story.

Can we be okay with walking alongside someone who continues to reject the message of Christ?

In this encounter, unlike the conversation with the woman at the well, "Jesus was content … to send this man away without the message of the gospel. Instead of the good news of salvation, Jesus leaves this teacher with some issues to ponder in his heart."[3] Doing this is only possible if we really believe that God is the one who saves. We must allow the Holy Spirit to do the work. Evangelism is what we are all called to do, but it is the ministry of the Holy Spirit and we are invited to join into that work.

Can we be okay with walking alongside someone who continues to reject the message of Christ? I'm sure that Jesus desperately wanted this man to leave behind the debate and genuinely follow after God. Could it be that Jesus knew the expert in the Law was not ready to receive the gospel? I know non-Christians that seem unready to know the gospel, but do I trust that God will provide a time for that to happen, whether I am the one to be there or not?

The Multiplication Method

As stated in the previous section, the personal evangelism moment with the woman at the well quickly turned into the multiplication method when she ran back to her town to share about her encounter with Jesus. At times, the multiplication method is seamless, like in this story. The new believer cannot contain the good news they have now heard. They automatically begin to share their story with anyone who will listen. In other instances, however, new believers need to be discipled in their new faith and helped to see their role in evangelizing and discipling others. For the multiplication to continue, new believers need to embrace their own call of spreading the good news of Jesus.

"*Each One Win One*" is a term that some of our own Nazarene leaders, Stan Toler and Louie Bustle, used in their guide to evangelism.[4] However, if we stop here we are just engaging in the addition method of evangelism, where every current believer has the task of making one more believer. Instead, every believer both current and new must fully embrace the call to share the Good News. That is why Toler and Bustle wrote a complimentary guide called "*Each One Disciple One*" where they resource leaders with tools for helping new believers grow in their faith and help them reach a place where they are ready to also share their faith with others.

We see a powerful example of the multiplication method after the death of Stephen in Acts 8. As the believers from the church in Jerusalem fell under persecution and were scattered, they continued to preach the Word wherever they went. They didn't wait for the apostles. Each believer accepted the responsibility of sharing the Good News with their new neighbors.

Group Evangelism

When we look at the early church, we see the first Christians sharing the good news of Jesus through both large group evangelism and small group evangelism. Acts 2 begins with the story of Pentecost and the bold message Peter proclaims to his fellow Israelites. Standing with the other apostles, he publicly declared Jesus to be Lord and Christ. Scripture records that 3,000 people believed what Peter said, were baptised, and entered into the community of believers that day.

While group evangelism is not strictly the responsibility of individuals (as in personal evangelism), it is a task for the entire church, the whole Body of Christ. Evangelistic rallies and campaigns, outreach events, cell groups, youth groups, special outreach such as prison, hospital, and rehab ministry, and even Sunday services are part of group evangelism. The danger, however, is when we begin to believe that group evangelism is the job of the pastors, the "Peters," or the apostles; those who can stand up and preach to large crowds. This is the furthest thing from the truth!

The end of Acts 2 goes on to tell of the smaller groups of believers: those who "devoted themselves to the apostles' teaching, to the community, to their shared meals, and to their prayers" (Acts 2:42). These groups of believers sold their possessions to support anyone who had a need and "every day, they met together in the temple and ate in their homes. They shared food with gladness and simplicity" (Acts 2:46). Through their faithful and self-sacrificing love for their brothers and sisters, "they praised God and demonstrated God's goodness to everyone. The Lord added daily to the community those who were being saved" (Acts 2:47). We must, like the early church, incorporate evangelism into every part of the "on-goings" and "out-goings" of the church.

Our Commission

The blueprint for evangelism is given by Jesus in Acts 1:8 and in Matthew 28:18-20:

> "But ye shall receive power, after that the Holy Ghost is come upon you: and ye shall be witnesses unto me both in Jerusalem, and in all Judea, and in Samaria, and unto the uttermost part of the earth."

> "All authority in heaven and on earth has been given to me. Go therefore and make disciples of all nations, baptizing them in the name of the Father and of the Son and of the Holy Spirit, teaching them to observe all that I have commanded you. And behold, I am with you always to the end of the age."

These two commissions bear a remarkable similarity to the very first command given by God in Genesis 1:28: "Be fruitful and increase in number, fill the Earth." This consistency of message says that since the beginning, we have had the task of filling the world with followers of Yahweh. More specifically, we see four distinct objectives in the Great Commission: going, making, baptizing, and teaching.

We need to view evangelism with the same creative lens we see Jesus and the early Christians employing.

"Going" instructs us to take the initiative to depart from where we are and reach out to those who are still seeking. We cannot afford to passively wait for the lost to come to us, as many churches have fallen into the mistaken habit of doing. We are asked to go to them. Biblical evangelism, or rather Christlike evangelism, is about reaching out, *going* to the lost of this world.

"Making" instructs us to preach and proclaim the Gospel as well as the effects of the Cross, grace, repentance, and faith. Evangelism is proclaiming to the world the cross of Christ, that He died for us, was buried, and rose again on the third day. Through this, we lead people to the point of confession and repentance. The word "make" is used instead of "preach" because it is not only the message but the Word made flesh, which was with God in the beginning, that we are introducing to the world. We are also sharing the promises and demands of believing in Him.

"Baptizing" instructs us to guide and call people from the stage of confession and repentance to the stage of professing our faith in Christ. Baptism is a means of grace which Jesus commands for every believer who receives the Gospel.

"Teaching" relates the importance of believers being grounded in the fundamental truths of God's Word. Once a new believer is baptized, they must receive continuous guidance on the principles and practices of Christian life. This is part of the "perfecting" of believers that we as Nazarenes call entire sanctification.

Our Role

Paul's first letter to the church in Corinth contains a key lesson regarding the various roles needed in the work of evangelism. While Paul is rebuking the believers, who are dividing off into sects based on the leader they came to faith under, Paul highlights the different roles we all might play along a person's journey to faith.

> "After all, what is Apollos? What is Paul? They are servants who helped you to believe. Each one had a role given to them by the Lord: I planted, Apollos watered, but God made it grow." (1 Corinthians 3:5-6)

As mentioned earlier in this chapter, sometimes we are the one who tills the soil, sometimes we plant the seed, sometimes we water the seeds, and sometimes we gather in the harvest. While God is always the one who does the critical work of making the seed grow, we should never dismiss or downplay our role at any given moment.

As youth workers we have a responsibility; not only to faithfully live out this calling in our own lives but to help our youth embrace this same calling. We need to view evangelism with the same creative lens we see Jesus and the early Christians employing. We need to move past a single model of a preacher on a street corner as the only way we think or talk about evangelism. We need to let go of guilt and prayerfully seek what God is asking of us.

CHAPTER 2

As You Begin: Developing the Correct Heart and Posture for Evangelism

Denise Holland

Denise Holland serves as the director of youth ministries at Brantford Church of the Nazarene in Brantford, Ontario, Canada. Youth ministry excites her because she is able to share Jesus and watch youth find Him. Evangelism is important to her because she wants everyone to have a chance to know Jesus' love and walk in the best relationship with God and others.

Do I really believe God and what His Word says? Do I believe that the human soul is eternal and that only those who receive Jesus' gift of salvation through faith in Him are going to heaven? Do I believe in hell, a place of eternal separation from God? These are questions I wish I had asked myself before my friend Mark died during our final year in university.

At the age of 23, when I thought I was invincible and had plenty of time to get things "right" with God, one of my closest friends was suddenly gone into eternity — the problem was, I wasn't sure where. Frantically, I began searching for answers to the deep questions of life and death with God and others. Questions like: where was my friend now? I was deeply disturbed by the possibilities. From what I had learned in church growing up, my friend, who didn't profess faith in Jesus, was in hell, separated from God for all eternity. I couldn't bear this thought! Not just because I loved my friend and could imagine him suffering intense pain, but also because I believed on some level it was my fault for not sharing the knowledge I had. I knew we must repent and trust in Jesus' death on the cross in order to be "saved" and have eternal life with God.

The weight of loss was crushing because I could have potentially been a part of helping my friend know God. Only God knows for sure if someone has faith, but the not-knowing-for-sure brought tremendous pain and guilt to my heart. Mark's death also brought me to some serious personal soul-searching. Was I ready to go to heaven and meet God when I died? Did I really believe humans are lost and going to an eternal hell without Jesus' salvation? If I did believe that we are lost without Jesus, then what was I doing wasting time keeping this knowledge to myself? I knew God was real and I knew Jesus was the only way to heaven, and yet I hadn't shared it because of fear. I cared more about what people thought of me than about being obedient to God. Before this, I had rarely reflected on mine or my friends' mortality and eternal destiny. I knew I had lost my moment to be a part of changing Mark's story, and I could never go back and fix my mistake! In my distress, however, I reached out to God for mercy and decided that from that point on I would live for God and with the Holy Spirit's help, I would be intentional about telling others about Jesus and what He did to save us.

In the book *Follow Me*, David Platt says:

> "What's most tragic is that we could be experiencing God, but instead we are experiencing guilt! Our fear of following Him into a life spent making disciples leaves us feeling disappointed in ourselves. Don't you struggle with this kind of guilt? You read the Bible and believe that Jesus is the only way to heaven. You fear that those who die apart from Christ face a horrifying future. Yet, for whatever reason, you've made little effort to warn your family and friends. You have neighbours, coworkers, and others who pass by daily without saying a word to them about Jesus. You look at your life and think, this doesn't make sense! Either I don't really believe the Bible, or I'm extremely unloving. I'm more concerned about being rejected than I am about someone else's eternal destiny.'"

Nothing Happens Without God and Prayer

David goes on to suggest that the answer to this complacency is to reject comfort and ease; to repent and be changed. We can't do anything of lasting value in ourselves. The book of Acts shows many examples of those who were empowered and led by the Holy Spirit. The Spirit enabled them to be effective witnesses, gave them boldness, and even demonstrated signs and wonders through them. Once we have received Christ and are filled with the Holy Spirit through repentance and faith, we must pray and ask for God to give us all we need to do this work of evangelism. Prayer opens our heart to the One who can do all things and acknowledges our own inadequacy and dependency on God for everything. This is the correct posture to begin sharing Christ with others.

When I went through that time of soul searching, I began looking at my own life and how desperately lost I was, trying to live without Christ. The first thing I did was to stop living my own way and surrender my life to God. I repented of my lack of faith, my willful disobedience to God, and confessed my desperate need of Jesus as my Saviour.

Then I began to pray for myself, because frankly, I was afraid! I felt so inadequate for the great task of sharing the Good News. I was afraid that

I wouldn't say the right words or remember the right Bible verses to tell people. I was afraid of being rejected by people who would think I was crazy or dumb for believing in God. I felt somehow like I was bothering people with what I had to say because they *seemed* perfectly happy without God. I prayed that God would give me a heart of love like His for people. I prayed God would give me His wisdom. I asked for God's Holy Spirit to go before me to prepare people's hearts and present opportunities for me to speak to people about salvation. I asked the Holy Spirit to em-power me to speak boldly and give me the right words before I went to visit people and that He would open their hearts to receive Him. Then, fearfully, I took the step of actually trusting God and began telling people about what Jesus had done for the world in order to give us new life and freedom from sin and death.

Prayer opens our heart to the One who can do all things, and acknowledges our own inadequacy and dependency on God for everything. This is the correct posture to begin sharing Christ with others.

The first time God opened the door for me to share my faith, I totally bailed. I planned what I was going to say in my mind as I was meeting with a dear friend that day. My heart was beating like crazy, but I got too scared and didn't say a thing. That night, I could not sleep. I kept thinking about my friend and what I should have said. I felt like a failure, like I was the weakest Christian ever. I prayed through the night and asked God to help me have courage and the right words to share. The first thing the next morning, I called her and said, "I have to meet you for coffee today. I was supposed to tell you something yesterday and I didn't and I couldn't sleep at all last night." At our meeting, with a red face and a heart palpitating so fast I thought I might pass out, I shared the good news of Jesus with my friend. She kindly heard me out, said "thanks" and that was it. I survived! Even though I felt it was the most awkward presentation of the gospel of all time, it was the most exhilarating feeling to know that I had obeyed God. I had pleased my King by doing His will. I was so happy that my friend had heard God's truth, even if I was dis-appointed that she didn't receive Jesus as her Saviour in an obvious way. Nonetheless, I knew she had all the information she needed to do just that.

Next, I had made a prayer list of everyone I could think of that wasn't yet in relationship with God and I prayed for the Holy Spirit to work on their hearts and minds, to put people in their lives who would share His salvation plan with them, and that I would be a living witness of Jesus to them through the life I lived and the words I spoke. I really wanted everyone to enter into relationship with our loving God and become new creations. I wanted them to hear my pastor speak and become part of a church family. I wanted them to read God's Word and discover Jesus for themselves. The prayer list has changed over the years as some people have entered into relationship with Christ; there are others I am still praying for. As I started praying for these things and followed through in sharing the words God put on my heart to say to people, God continued working and moved their hearts either to a new understanding of Himself, or to a place of acceptance. I was full of fear when I shared Christ's salvation with friends, but God overcame my fears as He showed Himself faithful every time. God gave me courage and, through His Holy Spirit, He moved in those people's lives to bring understanding and acceptance. After the first few experiences of sharing the gospel, I didn't feel so alone. I actually felt God with me, strengthening me each time and even giving me words to say that were not my own. I know He will do the same for you.

Most people I talked to about Jesus were not ready to go to church at first, but they did want to know more about God and what the Bible said about God. God gave me the idea of having a home Bible study with them. I had never led a Bible study before and I was afraid to mess it up, so I asked a friend if they would be willing to lead it and they agreed. Little did I know that God was preparing me to step out in faith and lead the study myself. The person who started the study could no longer lead after a couple months. I knew my friends were comfortable with me, so in faith, I took over leading the Bible Study. For the next two years I led them through a few different study books that helped us learn more about God and the Bible. As a result of our invested time with God, two dear friends received Jesus as Saviour and began attending church. Here is what I learned through this experience: people need time and a safe place to contemplate and grow before risking being part of the larger church community. Some individuals may take a long time before they surrender their lives to Jesus, and as heart-breaking as it is, others may never accept Him. As you share the Good News with others, remember that obedience to God is the measure of success, not the number of people who accept Christ. If you measure success by numbers, it's possible to become discouraged and quit or become arrogant instead of giving God glory.

People need time and a safe place to contemplate and grow before risking being part of the larger church community.

You, dear youth leader, are uniquely shaped to serve God in a one-of-a-kind way for which He has created you. Specifically asking God to reveal His heart for the lost will motivate you to action. Before you share the message of salvation with someone, you should ask to be empowered and given boldness through the Holy Spirit, asking Him to prepare the lost person's heart to understand and receive God's message of grace. Ask God to use you and your church community to implement His plans and dreams for you to share the gospel with those around you. As Oswald Chambers wrote, "The idea is not that we do work for God, but that we are so loyal to Him that He can do His work through us."[2]

In our setting, we wanted to reach out to teenagers (and their families) that did not know Christ or belong to a church body. We knew that in our area of the world (Canada), people were not just going to walk into a church building and ask to hear about God. We speculated that the reason was because it is intimidating when they have no background with the Church or Christianity and don't believe the Church has the answers they are looking for. We understood that we would have to build relationships with the youth in order to share Jesus, whereas most cold-calling evangelism doesn't give us opportunity for discipleship or relationship building. We believe God gave us the dream of having a youth drop-in centre. This would be a place of "neutral ground" outside the walls of the church building where our "church youth" could invite their friends who didn't know Christ and where unbelievers would feel comfortable. We wanted to create a space where our leaders could get to know the youth by spending time with them in a place filled with fun and intentionally "unprogramed" options. This allowed the leaders to put their energies into getting to know the youth rather than maintaining a program. As the community youth got to know the leaders, they began to trust us and share their lives with us. We intentionally made every opportunity to share our faith in Christ with them. Our Christian youth and leaders tried to model our faith through our interactions and expectations. We shared God's Word, wisdom, and answers to the real-life situations the youth told us about. By God's grace, some of these youth came to faith in Jesus. Some are undecided but continue to seek, and others have left but with seeds of God's truth planted in their hearts. We trust that one day, God will bring those seeds to fruition in a willing heart.

Without God and prayer, we were powerless to bring change in anyone's life, but God has done what we could not do.

Often, we have wondered: what if we never began the youth drop-in? We think of the hundreds of youth we have been able to share the love of Jesus with, care for, and be "the church" to. Youth who, otherwise, may have never heard the truth. We have been running the centre for eight years now, and it almost feels common place, but it's not. It is a miracle that God is working out in the lives of the youth, their families, and our lives. I assure you, *none* of this would have happened without prayer and God's faithfulness to work through our obedience to actually share Christ with the lost. He gave us the courage, wisdom, and resources to pursue the idea in the first place. He brought youth to the youth drop-in in various ways over the years. When we prayed for the youth to experience the Holy Spirit's drawing and for God to bring them to faith in Him, we had our prayers answered in many of them. Without God and prayer, we were powerless to bring change in anyone's life, but God has done what we could not do.

Join with Others

God never meant for us to do this alone. As you begin, make sure you have your church family's prayer support and join with other believers who are passionate about evangelism. If you are new at sharing the gospel, find other believers who are good at sharing it, learn from them, and practice with them. When I started sharing my faith, I had actually not witnessed anyone who did this. While reading God's Word, it was so evident that we as followers of Christ should be sharing the Good News that I felt compelled to try it just as God's Word commanded. I began by praying and sharing as much as I knew.

Later at a conference, I took an evangelism course with a man named Cory McKenna. He was teaching people to share their faith and then took them out to the streets of the city and modeled how his team did this. After we had prayed and asked God to use us and protect us, he gave us an opportunity to share what we had learned with individuals on the street that very day. We also had a prayer team back at the conference praying for us the whole time we were out sharing. Whether you go to a conference, read books about evangelism, or watch videos on the topic, as Nike says, "Just do it!" It's important to practice evangelism yourself. Practice may not make us perfect at evangelism, but it does make it easier and easier for us to share without so much fear and personal resistance. This happens as we experience the Spirit of God working through us and see God setting others free.

Remember, there are many different methods to share His message. No two people will do it exactly the same way. As you find your voice, don't be afraid to start small, it's just important that you start. I love the verse, "Do not despise these small beginnings, for the Lord rejoices to see the work begin" (Zechariah 4:10). You can join with others in what God is already doing in your area to reach the lost. If there is no one doing evangelism in your area, pray for direction, and ask God to show you how to start doing it yourself.

Ask God to send others to help you who love Him and have a desire to reach the lost: "Ask the Lord of the harvest, therefore, to send out workers into his harvest field" (Matthew 9:38). After you have prayed, step out in faith and share Christ with someone. Just watch how God works through you as you are obedient to Him. Much like our youth drop-in centre, you never know what can be accomplished for Christ unless you start.

Ask others to pray for you and those you are witnessing to. Before we began the youth drop-in, we asked our church family to pray for God to use us and this little place to bring people to faith in Him. As youth began to come, we gave a list of their names to the congregation to pray for each individual. This is one of the ways we can join with others in the great work of God. The evangelist is empowered by the striving of God's people in prayer for God to act on our behalf in a way we cannot do on our own. Those praying are a part of the work of evangelism as they cry out to God, who is at work in the lives of the lost. Remember, you are not alone. God, who called you and asks you to do this work, is with you. Those you ask to join with you in prayer are working in the spiritual realm on your behalf and on behalf of those with whom you will share Christ.

Commit to Obedience

Often, we look to the number of people who have received Christ as our indicator of success when sharing the gospel. However, our success is measured in being obedient to God.

Sharing the Good News with even one lost soul is of infinite value. Sharing the Good News is the success — not whether a person came to faith by what you said. You were faithful. You obeyed Christ. You planted a seed. The rest is up to the Holy Spirit and that person. There is more rejoicing in heaven over the one sinner who comes to repentance than over 99 of us who already believe. God's heart, and therefore our hearts, should be seeking the "one" by praying, sharing and discipling. It is not the number of souls who will attend a youth centre or church that should be our focus but doing what God asks us to do. Christ will build His church. He will draw men and women to Himself, and He will use us in that work.

We, as Christians, are God's instruments to carry out His will on earth. It's not just pastors, prophets, and theologians who are called to share the Good News and disciple people. It is all who have repented and turned from their ways to God's ways who are called to be part of His mission to seek and save the lost. God will equip us to do His will. "But we have this treasure in jars of clay to show this all surpassing power is from God and not from us" (2 Corinthians 4:7). As you dwell in Him, God will lead you where He wants you to go, to the people He has for you to reach, in a way that is best for your community.

Daniel Latu

Daniel Latu is the Melanesia & South Pacific Field Youth Coordinator and a pastor who serves in Suva, Fiji Islands. Youth ministry excites him because he can see God's purpose lived out in the next generation. He calls young people a "sea of Kingdom greats." Evangelism is important to Daniel because everyone is a big deal to God; we all matter.

In the Philippines — Metro Manila to be exact — a thriving motocross ministry gathers on a weekly basis. There is open space with marked motocross race tracks attracting motorcycle and extreme sports enthusiasts, passersby, and any curious onlookers. In the actual race setting, the riders (in full dirt bike gear) are racing around doing twists and turns and any other daredevil move possible. Here is the interesting bit: this is all part of an actual Sunday service. Yes, you read right, and like any other church service, it involves the whole family. The Word is preached, lives are prayed for, and there is an ongoing Bible study group among other exciting activities.

This is the ministry God planted in the heart of Pastor Sam Tamayo, a dynamic servant leader within the Church of the Nazarene and mentor to many young people. When I first visited the Philippines in October 2013, I had the pleasure of meeting Pastor Sam and his fellow ministry partner, Pastor Jordan Escusa, for the first time. Soon after the youth service, we sat for a meal at a popular burger joint and talked about youth ministry.

They passionately shared how this motocross ministry evolved; from early conviction, to making moves of faith in order to be where the people are, to dealing with all forms of challenges — all whilst simultaneously recognizing the steady growth that followed. I recall being in awe of two things as they shared. First, the phenomenal and awe-inspiring nature of God, and second, the faith and trust Pastor Sam put in God and the new move God birthed in him.

If we simply trust God for the steps He marks out for us and *just let God be God in the process*, it is incredible what the Lord will work out of our lives in the endeavors He leads us in. After all, He has us covered.

Bringing this story, and others like it, to the fore is to deal with the underlying reality of what happens when we are called to individuals or a people group we may not initially know. Mixed emotions of joy, reluctance, and insecurity may overwhelm you when you are called to such a task. Most times we are in awe of the results or the fruit of going to where the people are. The results are great, and we should celebrate them, but we also need to acknowledge and appreciate the deposit phase. This is the phase when almost nobody is able to support you, limited aid is available, and yet you are carrying a huge conviction from God to initiate something that is way *out of your comfort zone.*

The reluctance, the insecurity, the need to leave your comfort zone, all of this is what you and your youth group must deal with before making the move to go where the people are. When fear threatens to stop you, it can help to seek out a better understanding of your community. Take the camera off of you and look at your community. Look at the world we now live in. When we see the needs and trust that what we do will affect others, then our fears, insecurities, and comfort diminish in importance.

I pray that we reconcile the struggles within us against the realities around us and resolutely decide to make a difference. As a flourishing ministry, Nazarene Youth International strongly believes we are called to a dynamic life in Christ. We must expect that God will unleash great things that neither you nor your youth group think possible. The question then becomes, are you willing and ready to let God work through your life? Are you willing to follow God to where the people are and foster genuine relationship with them?

Given the broad audience, the purpose of this write-up is not to tell you exactly how to do relational evangelism. In whatever part of the world you are reading this piece, I will leave that discovery to you. Rather, the goal is to grant you an understanding of what relational evangelism is about and what makes it unique and effective. We will explore biblical principles that not only give voice to relational evangelism but are practical across our varying contexts. Consider this a launch pad designed to help you take off into your own journey of relational evangelism. In as far as your going is concerned, get excited in God. I guarantee that you will discover and learn so much more in the journey with Him than you would in any classroom or book.

Called For Such A Time

We have been uniquely gifted by God to serve our generation for a time like this. General Superintendent Dr. Carla Sunberg nailed it when she said:

> "For the survival of the church, we desperately need our young people. We need their passion, excitement, and vision for the future."

She is, without a doubt, correct. It is not so much that we are young — though that is important — but deeper still that God has deposited in us raw abilities He can use to birth new and creative ways for winning the lost, edifying the church, and glorifying His name.

When You Go — Timeless Lessons from The Past

This next story models the passion and excitement in a young person who is possessed by a vision for the future and who ventures out in faith to fulfill that vision with little support. It is the story of someone extremely committed to going to and getting to know the people God had called him to serve.

Born in 1882, Harmon F. Schmelzenbach lived his early years in the state of Texas, USA. A very unique individual, he was oblivious to how his influence would extend so far beyond the area where he was raised. He had a difficult childhood and was not exempt from trials. At age 12 he lost both parents, was taken in by another family, and pulled out of school to work. In his journey, he encountered the Lord Jesus and developed an intimate relationship with Him. As time went by, Harmon felt the nudge of God (calling, if you will) to Christian missions in Africa. This was in a time when Christianity was still unpopular in large parts of that area of the world. This was a mammoth task no doubt, but being strongly compelled of God, Harmon set sail when he was only in his mid-twenties on 18 June 1907 for Port Elizabeth in what is now South Africa.

What stands as extraordinary was that Harmon proceeded out of his comfort zone with a lot of belief and little help. Like Abraham, he sensed it was his time to move and trusted God as he took the first step of faith.

Active and passionate, Harmon led many to know the Lord Jesus Christ. He would eventually settle with his wife Lula in the present-day Kingdom of eSwatini, ministering to the people there. Despite the challenges, Harmon went above and beyond to get to know the people he was called to serve. He intentionally made it a priority to connect with the unreached, learn their language, and better communicate with them. He made every effort to learn the culture and the Swazi way of life. He did all of this while living with the ongoing death threats he received from those who opposed him. As Harmon developed relationships and was in community with the people, God transformed lives. Warriors who once called for his death were now his friends; a queen who rejected the idea of ever working with anyone white permitted Harmon to build a church on her land.

Relational evangelism is about going to individuals or communities and getting close to the people group God wants you to influence for His Glory.

Harmon was not the only person God called to serve in Africa. Many great men and women with unique stories like Harmon have each contributed to the church's work there. Today, the Church of the Nazarene on the Africa Region stands as one of the fastest growing church movements in our denomination.

It is worth noting that efforts like Harmon's come on the backdrop of a lot of faith in God and hard work, all enveloped in love.

At its core, that is relational evangelism. It is about going to individuals or communities and getting close to the people group God wants you to influence for His Glory, to build relationships and take genuine interest in them. It is different than famous open-air evangelism, the weekend crusades, or revival meetings. It takes time and requires a great deal of effort and a lot of commitment. As fascinating as it is, relational evangelism does present its own challenges — and, in the name of honesty, you will have your fair share of those — but take heart: God is with you in the journey.

As it was with those who lived out this legacy of God, it is our privilege to continue this Kingdom tradition. Not all of us will get the call to foreign missions or to begin a motocross ministry. For some, God may compel us to walk across the street to our neighbor's home or join the community teens at the park, sweating it out with exercises and sports. Maybe the opportunities will come through a friend at school, a co-worker, a relative, a book club, a sports club, common friends at a gaming center, or maybe farmers that you hang out with in the fields, herders, or folks like the apostle Peter who fish for a living — *the people and opportunities are plentiful.*

Be sensitive to the Holy Spirit's leading of your life. God sent Harmon, and today more than ever He is calling us to our world.

The Dark World

Embraced or not, the world needs Jesus.

Wherever you are, it really goes without saying that the world we live in needs saving, and not only a spiritual salvation. The way our multicultural societies are evolving on all major fronts — be it politics, economics, or health, among many others — gives little or less hope to the many affected. More and more people are deliberating whether things will turn out for the better. This sense of urgency to know how things will turn out is prompted by the insecurities flooding in from everything happening around us.

All disciples of Christ must know that the Great Commission is not optional. When we live out this command of Christ, we express the compassionate heart of our God.

Whenever you tune in to the many media broadcasts in your country or have an updated understanding of your own community or do a quick search about world news online, a majority of the news features are neither motivating nor positive.

We hear on the airwaves how these issues affect the perception and hope of many for a better life and community. Where I live, there is a general nostalgic response when talking to people about life — some will reminisce the past and conclude that these are not like the "good old days."

Hope in the Dark

The realities of these reports aside, we can still make a global difference. The entire world is our harvest field. It is crazy, and yes, it can be over-the-top, but it is still our harvest field. May the Lord burn in us an active passion to see the world saved. As John Wesley famously said, "I look upon the whole world as my parish."

Turning a blind eye to the needs around us will not resolve anything. On the contrary, the needs are only opportunities to spread the gospel of Jesus Christ. It is the way of Christ, it is the culture of His kingdom, and it is what BE.DO.GO is all about.

Some may disagree, but relational or not, evangelism is for everybody. Unless we are hermits, we are in constant contact with people every day. All disciples of Christ must know that the Great Commission (Matthew 28:18-20) is not optional. When we live out this command of Christ, we express the compassionate heart of our God. I pray you get involved. Our pioneer church leader, Dr. Phineas F. Bresee summed it this way: "We are debtors to every man, to give him the Gospel in the same measure that we have received it."

First Things First

1. Despite the examples given beforehand, Jesus Christ is our ultimate model. There is no relational evangelist as successful as Him. The principles He used are still relevant today. For it to be effective, relational evangelism must be a lifestyle and we best embrace that lifestyle by striving to be Christlike.

2. We cannot do God's business without God. Just as Jesus demonstrated, we need to have a daily, functioning, intimate relationship with God. If we skip this, whatever we do will result in failure. We have received the promised Holy Spirit and we need to be in tune with Him every day. The relationship we have with God helps us understand who we are in Christ. After all, we cannot give people hope if it is not real in our lives.

3. Be prayerful always for the opportunities, the individuals, and the people groups God wants us to get close to. Every person we will affect, every community we will impact, God already knows and He knows how to help us establish the connections. He already has the strategy for us.

4. Surround ourselves with people who are just as or more passionate, like-minded, and wiser than us in relational evangelism. We do not want to be the big fish in a small pond. Pray for God to connect us with those who challenge our understanding and model a life of Christlikeness, who will mentor and hold us accountable. There is great power in partnership.

5. Be willing to be vulnerable and desire a teachable spirit on the journey. God will broaden our creativity and renew our minds in the process. God may convict us to initiate something uniquely tailored to our people group that has never been done before.

6. Strive for integrity, and make sure we are people others can trust. If people cannot have confidence in us, then we discredit ourselves.

7. In any relationship, commitment is critical; it indicates intentionality on our part. Since relational evangelism is marked by building relationships, the success of our evangelism is dependent on how committed we are to those relationships. Commitment does not mean we get it right all the time. We are bound to make mistakes, but we must do whatever is necessary to tweak the problem and get moving forward. Don't give up. Keep trying. Press forward. That is commitment. Remember, it was Jesus' commitment which led to our redemption.

Going to Where the People Are

Unless the Lord shows us otherwise, we need not go far to impact or win someone over into the Kingdom. One of the most effective strategies for relational evangelism is to let God use our daily routine as a start. It does not matter whether we are high school or university students, a stay-at-home individual, or a worker in the office, the fields, yards, aboard ships and planes, etc.; wherever we are, God is able to use our ordinary, day-to-day life to initiate relational evangelism.

The key to relational evangelism is the word *relational*, which simply means to connect with other people. So in our going, we need to be prayerful and attentive to our interactions and how God is leading us.

Here is a Christlike example:

The narrative of Jesus calling His first disciples is one we should take careful note of. It has all the makings of relational evangelism. You can read of this encounter in Luke 5:1-11.

In the story, Christ enters the fishing community of Galilee. His ministry has just begun, and He has come to minister but also to call His disciples. Prior to meeting them, He has been healing the sick and rebuking demons out of the possessed. Here is the point: in His going, Christ availed Himself as a blessing. Whenever Jesus encountered a need, He attended to it. This became Jesus' life pattern, culminating in His death and resurrection for the saving of our lives.

In fact, after preaching by the Lake Gennesaret, Christ turned to Peter, and before calling him and the others to follow Him, He recognized their need for fish. These men had families to look after and had labored all night to catch fish but were unsuccessful. Once He identified the need, Christ provided for them.

It pays to recognize the need of the people around us and prayerfully consider how we can meet that need. It is an effective method that leads us into meaningful conversations with those whose needs we meet. We need to see ourselves as God's means of blessing "our world" to the people and the community around us. With that Christlike mindset, we will recognize the needs, and I pray it encourages us to do something about it.

Not all needs are monetary. If a student is gifted in a certain subject and their classmate is struggling, that is a need. Sometimes people just need someone to listen and talk to, or pray with, or carry the groceries. These kind gestures matter because they allow us to connect with people.

Of course, there will be those who will reject our offer. That is to be expected, but that is not our focus. We should never let obstacles stop us.

As we endeavor to be a blessing to those we interact with, eventually we will discern those with whom we ought to develop a more meaningful relationship. During the 2013 General Assembly, I met members of Reach 77, a ministry based in Chicago that strives to influence all of its 77 neighborhoods. Interestingly, in their exhibit booth they arranged a table, chairs, plates, cups, and cutleries. The group recognized that the sharing of a meal is an effective way of connecting with people. The table was the common ground where conversations were initiated and in the process of blessing many people with a meal, a few would ultimately inquire about the prayer before the meal and ask the hosts why such kindness was opened to them. This was the sign the hosts waited for to talk of Jesus and deepen the relationship.

Jesus healed and blessed a lot of people, but His twelve disciples were His core focus. Much of His time, effort, teachings, and energy were invested in them. For some of us, relational evangelism may begin with a single encounter. That, in itself, is a lot. Remember, if we are faithful with little, God will entrust us with much.

Incarnation — Doing Life

As these relationships develop, it is important that we do life with them. Over time we get involved in their lives and they get involved in ours — the good, the bad and the ugly episodes; these are part and parcel of doing life. We need to understand the people we are building relationship with and never rush the process. Let it take its course. Invite them to our youth group and willingly avail ourselves when they reciprocate.

Discover the Lord together.

There will be a part of this relationship where mentoring and disciple-making takes a deeper form, whether it is with us or some other trustworthy mentor that our newfound relationship is comfortable with. Consider this and be prepared. Jesus spent three years knowing His disciples and them knowing Him. In that journey, the disciples grew in their faith, understanding, and commitment to God. That did not exempt them from making mistakes or dropping the ball at some point.

As we do life with these individuals, understand that, like us, they too will make mistakes. Avoid being judgmental and know the difference between condemning and uplifting. In this process of journeying with a seeker or a new believer, we must strive to have a gracious presence. We can check with a mentor when we have doubts; they are there to guide us. Bear in mind, God is the only being that can change a life, and He is able to bring transformation.

One of your discoveries will be that this journey will impact and transform your life as well. Relational evangelism will take time, but in the process it does give us a two-way growth.

In this process of journeying with a seeker or a new believer, we must strive to have a gracious presence.

Love, Hope and Value

The underlying motive to all these stories, ministries, guidelines, and strategies is to affirm to our new friends that they are truly loved, that there is real hope in this world, and that they are valuable to God. Their lives matter just as ours do.

After all, when God, the greatest relational evangelist came to get you, He affirmed His love, granted you hope, and showed you your value. We are all worth the sacrifice of the King of Kings and every effort to bring another soul into the Kingdom is worth it. Everybody matters.

May God use you to make a difference in someone's life and be a blessing to your World. Lastly, and most importantly, all glory and credit belong to God only.

CHAPTER 4

Evangelism through Outreach: Opening Doors to Share God's Love

Christiano Malta

Christiano Malta is the South America regional NYI leader and a pastor who serves in Campinas, Brazil. Youth ministry is exciting to him because of the transformation and lifestyle changes seen in the youth. He sees evangelism as the Christian life speaking and believes that Christians need to have the Great Commission running through our veins.

Imagine unleashing more than 1,500 volunteers from 10 countries onto 13 key locations in one city. In October of 2016, as the leaders of the South America Nazarene Youth Conference, ALTITUD'16, we did just that. We partnered with Nazarene Compassionate Ministries in order to show the communities we served how the love of God breaks barriers of social class and nationality. Through this emphasis, called "Harvest Day," we shared God's love with nearly 2,700 people of all ages!

The idea of Harvest Day came from John 4:31-38, when Jesus tells His disciples to open their eyes because the fields are ripe for harvest. The larger context of this passage relates to a conversation Jesus has with His disciples where the disciples invite Jesus to eat, but Jesus replies He has food to eat that they do not know about. Jesus further clarifies by saying that His food "is to do the will of Him who sent me and to finish His work."

Two chapters later in John, we get a clearer explanation of what Jesus' work is when He tells the crowd "For I have come down from heaven not to do my will but to do the will of Him who sent me. And this is the will of Him who sent me, that I shall lose none of all those He has given me, but raise them up at the last day. For my Father's will is that everyone who looks to the Son and believes in Him shall have eternal life, and I will raise them up at the last day" (John 6:38-40).

In these two passages, Jesus is emphasizing the importance of full submission to the Father's will. By comparing the Father's will to His very food, Jesus is affirming the sustaining quality of obedience to God. Jesus' instruction to the disciples to "open your eyes and look at the fields! They are ripe for harvest" is a plea for them to recognize the urgency of sharing the gospel (John 4:35b).

Oswald J. Smith said, "Oh, my friends, we are loaded down with countless Church activities, while the real work of the Church, that of evangelizing the world and winning the lost, is almost entirely neglected."[1] When we look at the world, we can see the ripe fields. People are trying to fill the emptiness of their souls with things momentary and fleeting, but deep down it reveals the need of Jesus in their lives. With our eyes opened and seeing a field ripe for harvest, we created Harvest Day.

The focus of Harvest Day was to have an evangelistic impact. While we wanted to have a social impact on the community or neighborhoods we visited, we strove for opportunities to share the good news of Jesus as well. John Stott affirms that there is a partnership between evangelism and social action when he says, "social action is a partner in evangelism. As partners, the two belong to each other and yet are independent of each other. Each stands on its own feet in its own right alongside the other. Neither is a means to the other, or even a manifestation of the other. For each is an end in itself. Both are expressions of unfeigned love."[2]

People are trying to fill the emptiness of their souls with things momentary and fleeting, but deep down it reveals the need of Jesus in their lives.

It was critical for us to keep this partnership before us throughout the entire planning process. We could not rightly express the love of Christ if our only motivation for helping someone was to eventually have them pray a prayer. Likewise, we could not rightly help someone if we had no concern for introducing them to the restorative love of Christ. Therefore, with evangelism in one hand and social action in the other, there were various elements we considered in order to organize Harvest Day. I am going to focus on the consideration we needed to give to the location, finances, projects, date, spiritual preparation, logistics, and the local church connections. While a Harvest Day will likely look very different in your culture, all of these elements should be considered in the planning process.

Location

The first step in organizing a Harvest Day is to research and consider the possible locations to serve as project sites. In this study, it is necessary to consider four important points: social vulnerability, site logistics, visibility, and local church proximity.

Social Vulnerability: Social vulnerability "refers to a condition of material or moral fragility of individuals or groups in the face of risks produced by the socio-economic context. It is related to processes of social exclusion, discrimination, and violation of the rights of these groups or individuals, due to their level of income, education, health, geographic location, among others."[3] With the desire to have a social impact, attention should be given to identifying places in need of social aid. Consider the types of projects you anticipate being able to do and how they would match with the needs of each location being considered. If you can provide basic health care or dental cleaning and exams, then identify places in your area with limited medical and dental care access.

> **Whenever we do any kind of outreach project, we must think about the follow-up to that project and what comes next for the people we interact with.**

Site Logistics: It is important to know the capacity of the sites being considered. This will make it easier to decide the number of volunteers, types of projects, and amount of equipment most suitable for each site. For example, with our projects, some sites only had enough space to receive about 30 volunteers, while others received 80. Note whether meals can be provided on-site or if they would need to be brought in. This might determine whether a full-day or half-day project is planned for a given site. What are the transportation options? What equipment, tables, or chairs are available? Gathering all of this information at the beginning will help make sure that the project organized for a given site will fit with the support it is able to provide.

Visibility: It is necessary to have a place with an open area for the main activity of the project. The location should provide easy access to the people who live in the area, such as parks, schools, or other well known points in the community. It will be much easier to invite people to your event if it is in a well-known location. Additionally, a place that is highly visible will draw people in once the event starts.

Local Church Proximity: Whenever we do any kind of outreach project, we must think about the follow-up to that project and what comes next for the people we interact with. Our outreach demands a continuity in the lives of those who are reached, and this is really only possible through a local church in the region. If you are considering a site that is not close to a local church, consider meeting with the district superintendent to see if there are plans for planting a church in that area. Work in advance to see if the project you want to do would be a good fit with the church planting work. In the end, however, there must be a plan for follow-up and a pastor or group of believers who will be responsible for providing ongoing discipleship and support.

Finances

The second step in organizing a Harvest Day is to create a financial plan. Identify where the financial support for the event is coming from. Are local churches taking up offerings to support this outreach event? Are there business owners who are willing to donate some of the supplies? Remember, a big budget is not necessary in order to organize a Harvest Day. If you don't have funds to do big projects, then be creative and only choose projects that won't require much financial investment. Challenge your youth to come up with ways to raise money. Either way, identify how much money you will have to work with and divide it between the sites in an intentional and planned way. Our budget was based on the studies of the sites and the finances were allocated to each area according to the corresponding needs. It is good to revisit the budget once the projects have been identified to determine if any adjustments should be made, but completing the budget prior to choosing the projects will help guide the planning process towards projects you can afford to do.

Projects

The third step in organizing a Harvest Day is to identify the projects that should be included at each project site. You know your own community and culture best, so get a group of youth and leaders together and dream about what you can do. Include the information gathered during your location research regarding social vulnerability and site logistics to inform the types of projects being considered. A list of ideas for potential projects would be endless, but below are some projects we organized for Harvest Day along with some brief descriptions.

Street Art: This project focuses on the various forms of art which often attract youth; graffiti, theater, and dance. Build a couple of large panels 1 meter high by 3 meters long. On site, graffiti artists can begin to paint the panels while various theater and dance performances happen around them. You can pick a central theme that is woven throughout the various art forms, like God's love, forgiveness, mercy, etc.

Plant Trees: Some of the most worrying issues today are environmental concerns. Many urban settings would benefit greatly from having more trees. Consult with the public authorities to identify the best place for several new trees to be planted. Volunteers can work with professionals to make sure the seedlings are planted appropriately. A mass planting of trees will leave your mark on the city for years to come.

Hospital Visits: Work with local hospitals to identify the best times and appropriate ways to visit the patients. Prepare for the visits by selecting songs to sing and being prepared for someone to pray for the patients. If possible, take toys or flowers to give to the patients. Above all, make sure you are aware of any hospital protocols that need to be followed during the visit. Creating chaos or hindering the doctors and nurses in any way would be a damaging witness.

Morning Coffee: Set up a tent close to a bus stop or other high traffic area during the time when people are going to work in the morning and hand out cups of coffee. Write messages on the cups or find some other way to share a word of encouragement and blessing with them as they begin their day. Have enough volunteers present so some can step away if people want to talk more.

Outdoor Church: Have a church service outside the four walls of the church. Identify a busy, open space, and bring a group together to worship the Lord there. Include a time of worship, a sermon with a loving evangelistic message, and more worship with a time for people to respond.

Mega-Bazaar Benefit: Invite people to donate clothes and household items they no longer need and that are still in good condition. There are two groups that could be helped through the sale of these donated items. First, you should find a location close to where people would benefit from being able to buy clothes for little money. The main goal isn't to make a lot of money, but help people be able to buy needed items at a good price. Second, identify a charity or ministry that the money raised will be donated to. At the sale, announce what the charity or ministry is and that all proceeds will go to support their work.

Skate Park Outreach: Send your youth out into their own interest groups. Organize those who skateboard and go to a skate park to interact with the other skateboarders. Have some in the group who don't skateboard go along to watch and also to hand out bottles of water. Find a way to make it clear that some of the skateboarders are a part of the group handing out the water. You could all wear the same color hats or t-shirts or maybe have shirts with your ministry logo on them.

Football (Soccer) Tournament: Form an umpire team, a logistical support team, a registration support team, an awards team, and an evangelism team. Serve as the hosts for the tournament and spend the day facilitating the competitions. Plan for music, emcees, interviews with the players, and other fun activities to engage those attending. Throughout the day, the evangelism team will seek out opportunities to share the good news with the people who attend.

Elder Home Service: Work with the administrators of a care home for the elderly to organize a worship service for their residents. Plan the service for them, include worship, a message to encourage their hearts, and a time for listening to them share stories. See what needs the home might have, and if possible, bring a donation of money or of specific items.

Date

The fourth step in organizing a Harvest Day is to choose the date and times for these projects. Be strategic in choosing the date. We chose a weekend, but holidays are also good dates for many of these types of outreach projects. Make sure to be aware of any other activities happening at the same time which would impact the number of people you would be able to interact with and ultimately the goal of Harvest Day.

Spiritual Preparation

The next foundational element in preparing for Harvest Day is spiritual preparation. All of the projects mentioned above are good things to do, but they only become opportunities for encounters with the Almighty God if God is blessing the work and we are seeking the Holy Spirit's guidance and work among us and through us. The spiritual planning then is an intentional organization and preparation of intercessors from the very beginning of the project. These intercessors do the critical work of interceding for every event, team, volunteer, person that will be spoken to, soul to be reached, and the organizations and administrators that will be involved. This is not a side committee for the less engaged. These prayers are the keys for everything else we will do. In addition to regular or personal times of prayer, invite intercessors, organizers, and volunteers to participate in vigils, fasts, and other times of communal prayer in preparation for Harvest Day.

Logistic Planning

Once the foundational pieces are finalized regarding location, finances, and projects and the work is being covered in prayer, the next step is to begin the work of planning all the logistical details. This step in the planning is responsible for making everything possible, so don't try to do all of this by yourself! The size of the team you work with should increase along with the number of sites and projects being organized for Harvest Day.

There is not a specific checklist that could be included here because the logistical details will completely depend on where and what you are doing. However, here are some broad categories to consider while planning all of the logistics.

Advanced Instructions: If a project requires rehearsals, specific attire, or additional volunteer training, consider how and when those details will be communicated and arranged.

Meeting Site: Where will volunteers be gathering to be organized and receive instructions?

Transportation: How will volunteers get to and from their project site?

Project Supplies: What are all the supplies that will be needed for each project, and how will they be obtained, gathered, distributed, and delivered to each project site?

Volunteer Care: Are restrooms available to the volunteers at their site? Will they be at the site long enough to need food or water? If so, how will that be provided?

Partner Care: If a project involves partnering with another ministry or organization, what rules do they have? What rules do the volunteers need to be made aware of?

Site Care: Will trash bags, boxes, brooms, etc. be needed in order to leave the site in better condition than it was when the volunteers arrived?

This stage of planning benefits greatly from having more people involved. Have at least one person who is specifically responsible for each particular site. This person can focus on the unique challenges and needs of their site. Also, have times for all the site coordinators to discuss their plans as a group. Hearing the details of one site might help another site coordinator identify a need they had missed.

Remember, while spending time focusing on all the logistics might seem tedious and unimportant, being organized will allow everyone on Harvest Day to keep their focus on the true purpose of the day, which is to be available to the people so that the Good News is shared with them and God's love for them is made known.

Local Church Connection

As mentioned previously, sites should be selected based on their proximity to a church. The pastors or representatives from the local churches should be a part of the planning process from the beginning. These local leaders can help you make sure the project you are planning for their neighborhood really is a good fit and will connect with people in their area.

Each local church should have two key responsibilities. First, they should organize a group of volunteers to support the Harvest Day projects. It is important to have people from the local church at the project so that people who are reached through the efforts of Harvest Day can meet people who will be at the local church they will be invited to. Second, the local church should develop a follow-up plan to provide support, connection, and discipleship for those who come to know Jesus as their Savior at Harvest Day. Harvest Day will have little lasting impact if thought is only given to that one day. There needs to be a solid plan for helping these new believers grow and mature in their faith. This will be discussed further in the final section of this chapter.

Therefore, as Harvest Day approaches, it is necessary to meet directly with the local church, at least a week in advance, to review all the details regarding schedules, activities, neighborhood evangelism, church community activities, and other action-related issues. Confirm the plans for church members to be present and review the follow-up plan.

Harvest Day Mission

After everything is planned, look forward with great expectation and readiness to a supernatural move of God in your midst, in the community, and in the local church. For us, Harvest Day was a significant moment as we saw lives being saved and people being impacted by the gospel.

As I close this chapter, here are some final thoughts to keep in mind when doing any type of evangelism through outreach events.

Contextualization: As I mentioned at the beginning of this chapter, not all of the project ideas will work in your culture, so contextualize the general concepts. Dream of ways your youth can respond to the needs of those around you. Think creatively of fresh ways to share God's love with the people in your city. Get a group of dreamers and creative thinkers together with your youth. Start by making a list of needs in your city. From there, start to come up with ways to respond to those needs. Continue by coming up with ideas of things you could do to bring a smile to a stranger's face. Keep the faces of your neighbors in mind throughout this whole process. Know your city and plan for your city specifically.

Sensitivity: All evangelism should be done with sensitivity towards and for those we seek to reach. This is even truer for outreach evangelism. We have to keep in mind that these people don't know us, might not know anything about God and the church, or might have hurts they carry that are connected to anything religious. This is why the spiritual preparation is so critical. When we step out to share God's light with a dark world, we are confronting more than just a lack of knowledge. Thus, when we interact with those we are serving or start a conversation with someone being drawn in by the activity around the project, we must be sensitive to them. Get to know them. Ask about their story. Ask about their hopes and struggles. Be sensitive to their story and to the Holy Spirit's leading as well. Listen for ways you see God at work already in their life and call their attention to that. This level of sensitivity communicates a genuine concern for them as a person, which is a reflection of how God sees them. Our goal is to share God's love, not to offend people in Jesus' name.

Listen for ways you see God at work already in their life and call their attention to that.

Follow-up: I touched on this briefly in the section discussing the connection with the local church, but the issue of follow-up deserves some more attention. Too often, evangelism through outreach events is seen as a stand-alone emphasis. There is a plan to share the Gospel with people in the community and once we go back to the church, we are done. We cannot do that! The Great Commission says, "Therefore go and make disciples of all nations, baptizing them in the name of the Father and of the Son and of the Holy Spirit, and teaching them to obey everything I have commanded you. And surely I am with you always, to the very end of the age" (Matthew 28:19-20). Jesus' instructions are to go and make disciples, not go and help people pray a prayer. Our responsibility towards someone doesn't end when we share the gospel with them; rather it has just begun. Be prepared with a way to collect the contact information of those who are saved. Provide them with information about the closest local church, including location and service times. Share a way to connect with key ministry leaders when they arrive at the church. Make sure they know they are invited to any of the discipleship programs the church has. Let them know you see this as a beginning of their journey with Christ and you are committed to walking along with them.

CHAPTER 5

Creative Evangelism: Thinking Inside the Box

Wouter van der Zeijden

Wouter van der Zeijden is a youth pastor who serves in the Netherlands. There is not much Wouter doesn't love about youth ministry. Some of his favorite things include hilarious games, good questions, friendships, reflection, growing, jokes at the last row in church, life-changing decisions, and not always knowing the answers.

No, No ... You Should Talk to My Wife

The sun is shining and the trees I can see from my study room are covered with a bit of snow. For the first time this winter, the channel beside my house is covered with a small coating of ice. The sheep in front of my house don't seem to be bothered by the cold temperature and are just standing there like every day. It's a rare peaceful view in the outskirts of just another suburb of a large city in the Netherlands.

Looking at the beautiful scenery outside helps me to sit down and relax a bit. The second I sit down, the big question pops up again which has been there since I was asked to write a chapter in this book about evangelism: "why me?"

You should talk to my wife about evangelism. She's the one who's easy with people, always chats with strangers in the train, while I prefer to just look outside the window and wander around in my mind. So, I'm a bit shy and don't really like to talk to strangers. Not a typical evangelist guy, I would say. Besides that, I like to work "backstage" — preferably all by myself. Nobody around me. Just me.

Somehow, I managed to get involved in a project during the last three years which brought me to the edges of my comfort zone concerning this evangelism thing. I had to work with a lot of people — not my style — with a main goal to evangelise. Definitely not my style. But the guy who came up with the idea for the project? Well, that was me.

How things work in the Netherlands

Let me share a bit about the country I live in. For those of you who don't really know a lot about the Netherlands, besides windmills, cheese, and that it's legal to use drugs, the Netherlands is a typical post-modern, post-Christian society, like most Western European countries.

Most people have a negative attitude towards large evangelism events or just any kind of evangelism. It's no problem being a Christian as long as it's your own personal faith and you're not trying to convince people to also become a Christian.

I'm 37 years old now, born and raised in the Church of the Nazarene. I love the church. I've been engaged with different kinds of youth activities all of my life. Over the last few years I've been our district youth pastor. All my friends, colleagues, and neighbors know me as a passionate Christian, but I guess working on this project still felt like coming out of the closet in a way. "Hi guys, we're Christians, I hope you don't mind."

Think Inside the Box

So, what's up with this project? Before I tell you all about it, I want to share how it all started. The main thing I hope to achieve with this chapter is not to inform you about just another project in some far away country, but to inspire you to think outside the box and start with your own idea. The key of success wasn't this awesome idea but that the project perfectly fits in "the DNA" of our church.

I don't know about your church or how you would describe "the DNA" of your church. I know my church is fairly big, especially for Western European standards, with about 800 members and a large crowd of people who look at the weekly broadcasted services and Bible studies. So, we have a large group of people who are passionate about broadcasting. We've got quite a bit of technical stuff hanging on the ceiling, and all members are used to having four cameras filming in the church during a service.

During one service our pastor challenged us to engage in youth work, and I was touched by his sermon. While sitting on my chair, I looked around, saw the cameras and thought, "It shouldn't be so hard to make a live broadcasted, late-night show for young people with all this stuff we have in here. We only have to remove the chairs, add a table, point the cameras at the table and … we're ready to go!"

If you take a look at the one of the episodes of Xperience TV now (www.xptv.nl) you will see it took a bit more than that. Actually, a lot more. We are very blessed with a church board who is willing to invest in young people and some very generous church members who gave extra funding for the project.

But … it would have never happened if I would have suggested to, let's say, start a sports project with young people or start a restaurant for poor people in our neighborhood. It's not in "the DNA" of our church. This is what we are good at. In a way, I didn't think outside the box, but I thought inside the box. We've already had some pretty cool stuff and some serious talents inside our "box." I combined them, added just a small idea (late-night TV program for young people), and the rest almost happened automatically.

So, before you read on, take a moment to think about your church. What defines your church? What are people passionate about? When you read more about Xperience TV, what could be your idea that will turn your church upside down?

Example: Xperience TV

With Xperience TV, we are building a bridge to the Church of the Nazarene for young people in our city. The show is like a late-night show full of music, fun games, interviews, and some serious thoughts we are sharing with the young people. We distribute the show on social media and invite young people to see the show live in the studio.

In a typical show we invite a talented band, not too famous (read: willing to perform for free), but large enough to already have a group of fans. I can clearly remember one TV show in which we invited a boyband where actually about a 100 screaming girls showed up, hours before we started, screaming to get into … church. OK, for them it wasn't a church; it was just a TV studio. But just imagine the picture. When was the last time you saw a 100 scream-ing girls just dying to get into a church?

That particular TV show itself wasn't so spectacular. The boyband did what they always do — sing a terribly bad song with doubtful lyrics — we played some games and we somehow managed to have a two-minute serious conversation.

Still, the best thing happened when the cameras stopped filming. We invited the girls for some more time of fellowship in our youth café. They somehow got touched by the nice atmosphere and the fact that they were fully accepted how they were.

That's the idea. After every TV show, our youth leaders invite all of the present young people for other activities like small groups and Bible studies. By doing that, they are the essential key in building a bridge to the church. Since we've started Xperience TV, we've seen our youth group double itself! The most interesting thing is that we didn't just find a way to get our own young people enthusiastic but also regularly see young people who don't know Jesus at all.

> **They feel loved. They feel they can be themselves and see people who care about them.**

In our monthly shows we see that "just" being at the show somehow seems to change young people. They feel loved. They feel they can be themselves and see people who care about them. We deliberately invite non-Christian young people into our production team so they get to see the real church. They will see we have arguments and miscommunications, but we also have forgiveness, respect, and love. We give them an insight in our lives while we work, eat, and pray. Through this shared time and insight, we see people slowly change, get interested, see how they can start to join other activities, build relationships, and along the way get to know Jesus more and more.

Confused About How God Works

When I grew up and joined Sunday School as a little boy, the idea of evangelism seemed pretty simple to me: a person who loves God is very enthusiastic and tells other people about God. With this project, I kind of got confused about what happened. After a while, a few of the boyband-girls I mentioned started coming more often and also joined our production team. Was God in some kind of strange way using these non-believing young people to reach other non-believing young people?

When I started the project, I had thought God would work mainly through the TV shows, but when I look back I see God was mainly working through the relationships. God seemed pretty far away during the boyband performance. But without it, one year later we wouldn't have had a conversation with one of the boyband-girls when she mentioned she just had a second abortion within one year. One other girl wouldn't have shared her story of her mum's boyfriend who would come out of prison in a few days hoping he would be a good new dad. I don't know what the leaders said at those moments, but clearly God was working through these intimate conversations.

So, before I continue, I'm asking you to completely forget about this whole TV show. It will probably be a very bad idea if you copy it and try to organise something like it in your own church. Think inside the box again. What's the DNA of your church?

Example: Glass House Project

One year after we started Xperience TV, we had an awesome opportunity for a new evangelism project. We started the Glass House Project.

The Glass House Project was organised by the crew of Xperience TV: a nonstop, 24-hour TV show in the center of Vlaardingen, full of music and hilarious challenges to raise money and awareness for "silent disasters." In a way it was a bit like a normal Xperience TV show, but now 24 hours long and not in our own studio, but on a big square in the middle of the city.

The initial plan was to organise the project at the parking lot of the Church of the Nazarene in Vlaardingen, being a small neighborhood project. After talking with the local government, we relocated the project to the center, turning it into a larger city project. The local government was enthusiastic about the project, which was pretty rare since it was organised by a church. Usually the local government isn't so enthusiastic to get related with churches.

Organising a huge *traditional* evangelism show would definitely not work in the Netherlands, but with the good experiences from our first season of Xperience TV we were encouraged to take it a step further. The project had multiple goals seen as "layers." The deeper you got into the project, the more you found out that we had a deep desire to tell people about God's love for them.

1. **Raise money for a "silent disaster" in the world.** The Glass House project is a well-known project in the Netherlands. It's organised by a secular radio station and The Red Cross to raise money for "silent disasters" in the world. Everybody in the Netherlands is called to get in action and

start their own projects to raise money. We as Christians embraced this project and organised our own Glass House. It was a "little brother" compared to the big national event organised around Christmas. The goal was to raise money for the national event.

2. *Make people think about "silent disasters" in our own city.* During the 24-hour show, we challenged people to get in action for "silent disasters" in our city. For example: lonely elder people, single mums without any income, or refugees who just came to our city. Clearly stated, our belief is that it's good not to just be aimed at one's self, but that people will be happier if they share their love, attention, care, and money instead of just receiving it. We stimulated people to invest in one's neighbor and neighborhood. At this point, we mainly focused on a good, Christian, loving, and caring way of living but didn't pro-actively make a direct connection with it. We focused on social holiness and mainly tried to convince people to help people in need.

3. *Build relationships.* With the Glass House project we had the same philosophy as with Xperience TV. Everybody is invited to join the team. We accept them as they are and work with them on an amazing project. We pray, we eat, we struggle, and we forgive. Living a life like Christ as an example for them. We build relationships and invite them for our monthly shows.

The Girl with the Camera

It's been one year since we've organised the Glass House project. Every Sunday since, when I enter church I look at the camera positions. Will she be there? I look for the girl who knocked at the big window while I was sitting in the Glass House trying to stay awake after 24 hours of continuous hard work. "Can I help you guys?" I was a bit confused because the event was about to end. "No, not really … but if you like you can come to our TV show next month." "Okay, but I don't want to wait that long. Can't I help you earlier?" My mind wasn't working that fast after 24 hours of being awake and I don't really know what happened afterwards, but the next Sunday after the event she was sitting behind one of the camera's in our church. "You don't mind that I don't believe anything this old guy on the stage is saying, do you?" she whispered when I entered church. Do I mind? I don't know … I guess I can't expect that, but it would be nice of course, I thought to myself.

Remember to think inside the box first. I bet your church has this one thing most people are enthusiastic about.

A confused smile appeared on my face. At that moment, the "old guy on the stage" had just started to pray, giving me the ability to think a bit longer about my answer, but mainly to thank God for this girl being here.

One year later, she's still there almost every Sunday, just filming the old guy on the stage and giving me a big hug after the service. I see how God is working in her life and often remind myself that it was definitely worth all the preparations and energy, even if it was just for this one girl.

Being Smart: Connect with Your Existing Ministries

Speaking about a lot of work, I have to admit this Glass House Project was maybe a bit too big for us as a church. It cost a handful of people almost a day-job for a few months to get it all organised. Unfortunately, we weren't able to organise it the year after.

The Church of the Nazarene in Zaanstad was a bit smarter a year later. They also organised a Glass House project but organised it within their coffee bar connected to their church, locking up their pastors for seven days! People could come by, buy some coffee, and just have a chat with the pastors. Like in Vlaardingen, they were able to build relationships with their neighbours and all kinds of organisations within their local community. They were able to share God's love through that.

The best thing about Zaanstad is that they actually found a way to organise an event like this and make it very easy to repeat in the upcoming years by simply extending their coffee bar ministry a little bit. The Glass House concept was the same, but organising it was much simpler.

Church DNA: The Unique Qualities of Your Church

So, are you fired up to get started with a Glass House of your own? Don't even think about it. No, don't do it. Remember to think inside the box first. I bet your church has this one thing most people are enthusiastic about. It's the unique quality of your church. The DNA of your church.

Do you have a lot of teachers?
Start a ministry in homework assistance.

Are a lot of people running to stay fit?
Start a run-with-friends-and-eat-afterward ministry.

Are you located in the town centre?
Start a coffee-ministry.

Do you have a group of people who always go into the mountains?
Start a survival-ministry.

I think you get the point.

Think inside the box to get to awesome new outside-the-box ministries.

CHAPTER 6

Re-Evangelism: Reaching Those Overly-Saturated with Christianity

Dario Richards

Dario Richards serves as the Caribbean Field Global Missions Coordinator and senior pastor in Bridgetown, Barbados. Youth ministry excites him because of the opportunity to encourage young people to discover and pursue their purpose from an early age. The salvation of people is important to Dario. He sees evangelism as the primary avenue by which people are saved.

I was ecstatic about serving in a new culture and context. From the pre-trip meetings, the journey from my home, and the initial meetings on the ground, I was anticipating great testimonies of salvation. I envisioned walking around the neighborhood and sharing the Good News with the young men on the corner. I anticipated engaging the vendor on the side of the road and meeting with the housewife during the day to study the Scriptures. Each imagined encounter fueled my eagerness to share the Gospel and heightened my expectations of what God would do. However, after three days on the field, I was exhausted, frustrated, and ready to give up. My enthusiasm waned and my initial excitement of serving in a new context and culture was slowly replaced with depression. This was certainly not what I had anticipated.

As I reflected on my frustrations one night, I realized that they did not stem from the opposition and rejection I faced in response to the Gospel. It was not the closed doors, folded arms, or the "no thank you, I am not interested" that caused my enthusiasm to wane. Nor was it the exhaustion of walking tirelessly in the blazing sun with no one in sight to hear the message. Even when people heard the message and walked away with no desire to respond to the Gospel, I was still zealous about sharing the Good News the next day. It was not the opposition and rejection to the Gospel that made me want to give up; it was people's knowledge and acceptance of the Gospel that was disconcerting.

By now you are probably confused. You might be asking yourself why would I be depressed, exhausted, frustrated, and ready to give up if most people were accepting the Good News we were sharing? Wasn't that the point? Isn't it our objective as Christians to invite people to respond to the Good News and to accept Jesus as their personal Lord and Savior? Isn't that the goal? If so, what was my problem?

I believe that a true response to the Gospel requires more than a cognitive agreement that it is true. It demands more than being able to retell a story about a God who has a Son who died on a tree many years ago. In my opinion, being saved is not only demonstrated in church attendance or church affiliation. We are not saved because we read our Bible daily or pray as soon as we wake up and right before we sleep. Salvation is not even hereditary. We are not automatically saved because our parents or grandparents are saved, or we grew up in a Christian home. It is not an inheritance that is left to us in a will. A true response to the good news of Jesus Christ requires so much more.

Salvation is not only what we think or believe. Salvation is God's initiative of drawing us unto Himself (John 6:44), which is a gift from God that we cannot earn or purchase (Ephesians 2:8-9). However, although salvation is a gift from God, we also have a responsibility in living out our salvation. For this reason, Don Thorsen refers to salvation as being both a gift and a task.[1] In other words, salvation must result in our repentance and a decision to turn away from sin and walk faithfully in obedience to God. Salvation must be evident in our confession, new conviction, and continuous transformation into the image of God. Simply put, if we are truly saved, it cannot simply be evident in what we say or claim to believe, it must also bear fruit in what we do. In the words of John the Baptist, "we must produce fruit in keeping with repentance" (Luke 3:8).

So, let us return to my frustration. It seemed like every door I knocked on, there was another individual who claimed to be saved. However, with further inquiry, it was discovered that their "salvation" experience wasn't based on repentance that led to transformation through Christ. In many cases, persons considered themselves Christians because they believed God existed or because they attended church or were committed to daily prayer and Bible reading. I must interject here and clarify that in sharing the Gospel, we did not make snap judgments of a person's Christianity. It was during conversation with them, after they indicated that they were a Christian, that they revealed their Christianity did not extend beyond the trimmings of religiosity. They had no testimonies of conversion or acceptance of Jesus Christ as Lord and Saviour. For instance, one woman we met was convinced that she was a Christian because she went to Sunday School as a child and still prays and reads her Bible occasionally. Although she no longer attends church nor recalls choosing to accept Jesus as her personal Savior, she was convinced that her prayers and belief in God were enough to justify her salvation. "After all," she said, "I am not as bad as some people I know. I read my Bible, you know!"

As a missionary, the fact that so many people were deceived without any sign that they were interested in the truth was more frustrating than being rejected. What was even more depressing was that this wasn't the first time I had experienced this on the mission field. As a matter of fact, in my part of the world, this was a norm.

In many parts of the western world, there are countries that would be considered over-saturated with the Gospel. Christianity is so widespread in these nations, they are considered Christian nations. What is unfortunate about many of these places that are over-saturated with the Gospel is the emergence of a popular type of Christianity that isn't necessarily a biblical Christianity. In these contexts, what emerges is a more self-centered type of Christianity than Christ-centered; a more relativistic type of Christianity than truth-based. Wherever this happens, there are usually three major repercussions that emerge regarding the gospel: deception, desensitization, and damage.

Deception

Deception refers to the fact that people become convinced they are truly saved when they really are not. Not too long ago, we were evangelizing in a community in what would be considered a "Christian nation." As we walked around and introduced ourselves, we passed an area where a small crowd was gathered. Within this crowd, some were smoking marijuana, some were gambling, some drinking alcohol and cursing. When they became aware that we were standing there, one of the ladies in the crowd requested that we follow her home to pray for her ill mother. We obliged.

When we reached her house, a few persons went in to pray and encourage the elderly lady. However, my wife and I stayed outside and decided to share the Good News with the lady who had brought us. As we shared, the lady began nodding her head, acknowledging what was being shared and indicating complete agreement. At the end, when we called for a response to the message, we were very surprised to hear the lady confess that she was a Christian. In an effort not to be judgmental and assume that she wasn't saved based on what she was engaged in when we met her, we asked her to explain what she meant by "I am already a Christian." While pointing in the direction of the church, she responded, "I grew up in the church, I pray every morning, and I visit the church occasionally."

We remained with her for a while talking about Christianity and the Gospel. When we eventually left, we were in both shock and pain. Shocked because of how adamant the lady was that church attendance meant she was a Christian and in pain because the lady was deceived. As we reflected on this experience, we realized how many similar experiences we have had on the mission field, where affiliation with the church or growing up in a Christian context was equated with being a Christian. During our devotional sessions that night on the mission field, we prayed particularly for persons whose understanding of the Gospel or Christianity was not in alignment with the Word of God. We prayed God would open their eyes and heart to His truth and the truth of the Gospel. It does not matter how popular Christianity is in a culture, if the popular teachings of Christianity do not align with the Bible, then people will be deceived.

Desensitization

Another consequence to popular Christianity that is contrary to biblical Christianity is what appears to be the desensitization of individuals toward the Good News. In some countries, the Gospel is so popular; you can find it practically anywhere. It is taught in schools, shown on television, celebrated in the culture, and the list goes on. Many of these nations even have national holidays rooted in Christianity.

How could people know so much about God, the Gospel, and the Scriptures and still reject God's gift of salvation? Unfortunately, even though nothing is inherently wrong with the mass promotion of the Gospel, one of the results of this is the fact that the Good News just becomes another story added to an individual's library. It is not uncommon in some cultures to find non-Christians who can recite the Gospel better than some Christians. I have had several encounters with persons who openly admitted that they were not Christians and found pleasure in quoting the Scriptures and even recounting the Gospel for me. There were even times when such encounters left me questioning the power of the Gospel.

How could people know so much about God, the Gospel, and the Scriptures and still reject God's gift of salvation? I had begun to convince myself that the Gospel "won't work." This meant that I no longer expected anyone to respond to the Good News. I was literally knocking on doors and feeling as though my time was being wasted, because no one was going to accept Christ. After evangelizing for a few days and getting nowhere I felt like a failure.

One night while reflecting, I was reminded that despite the desensitization of the population, the Gospel was still the power of God unto salvation to anyone who believed (Romans 1:16). In that moment, I realized that the Gospel wasn't the problem, neither were the people, but that I was. People might have grown familiar to the message, but the Gospel hadn't lost its power.

Damage

Any individual who claims to be of Christ and tries to live in obedience to Christ but without the power of the Holy Spirit will be the source of much hurt and pain. Such frameworks create a level of expectation that are impossible to meet. Naturally, people come to the church expecting to receive what is taught in the Scriptures. Unfortunately, this sometimes results in a painful experience, because the "church" was simply incapable of meeting the expectations.

Many philosophers, theologians and apologists have concluded that we are now living in a "post-Christian" world. Post Christianity refers to the loss of the primacy of the Christian worldview in political affairs, especially in those countries where Christianity had previously flourished, in favor of alternative views such as secularism or nationalism.[2] It includes personal worldviews, ideologies, religious movements, or societies that are no longer rooted in the language and assumptions of Christianity — at least explicitly — although they had previously been in an environment of ubiquitous Christianity. In other words, it appears as though people in countries once considered "Christian nations" are moving away from Christianity at a noticeable rate.

It would not be fair to say that post-Christianity is solely the result of the hurt, pain, and apparent hypocrisy of the church in areas overly-saturated with the Gospel. However, it is one of the major reasons. Though deception is one reality that hinders the Gospel, there are also numerous experiences of rejection. In some instances, individuals are not necessarily rejecting God or the Gospel but rather rejecting the Church.

In his book *Gandhi: An Interpretation*, E. Stanley Jones shares the story of Mahatma Gandhi's struggle with Christianity and his ultimate decision to not become a Christian.

> *"It was not easy for him to decide to be a Christian in the race-heavy atmosphere of South Africa. How could he really see Christ through all this racialism? He did see Christ in C. F. Andrews ... when C.F.A. was to speak in a church in South Africa, Gandhi was not allowed to enter the church because ... the color of his skin was not white."*[3]

Stanley goes on to lament, "How could Gandhi see Christ through that? Racialism has many sins to bear, but perhaps its worst sin was the obscuring of Christ in an hour when one of the greatest souls born of woman was making his decision."[4]

These three consequences — deception, desensitization, and damage — pose as three of the major threats to the advancement of the true Gospel in contexts oversaturated with the Gospel. Hence, in many cases, there seems to be an exodus from the church, especially among young people. The result is that the church is losing influence and relevance in these contexts and is unable to maintain the impact it once had.

What Can We Do?

Though the Church has been able to accomplish a number of great things within countries oversaturated with the Gospel, it is evident that there have been a number of hindrances as well. It would be a shame for the Church to continue to sit idly by and watch as we lose a grip on the countries and societies where Christianity once thrived.

However, as the current state and reality is considered, one might wonder what can be done? How does the Church regain her progress and make an even greater impact within these countries than she initially did? How can the Church effectively re-evangelize these nations?

One thing is clear: the goal of re-evangelism will not be achieved by simply adding more programs and activities. The new approach in these contexts must be much less program-based and much more principle-based. The focus must be less on what can be done and much more on why it is being done. It becomes much easier to build effective programs as our principles are clarified.

Another reason for pursuing a principle-based approach is to ensure longevity. As the Church, we want to ensure that our impact lasts throughout generations, and this will primarily be achieved through the transference of strong principles. Programs must change and adapt to the time and culture if they are to remain relevant. However, principles remain fixed. They transcend culture and generations. Therefore, if principles are kept, the possibility of the impact being long-lasting is inevitable.

To this end, there are three major principles that must undergird everything the Church pursues: Christ-centered vision, holistic mission, and prayer.

Christ-Centered Vision

One of the major principles of success in the world of business and leadership is the concept of beginning with the end in mind. The idea is that whenever one is pursuing any goal, you must first be able to clearly define what that goal looks like. There must be a very clear picture of what the desired end result is. Leaders and thinkers call this picture vision.

By definition, a vision is a picture of a preferred future. It captures the destination of one's intended journey and keeps one's eyes fixed and focused. Similarly, if the Church is going to be successful in re-evangelism, there must be a clearly defined picture of what we intend to achieve.

From the beginning to the end, the centrality of Christ must be critical in every endeavor and must serve as the only mark of success in evangelism.

This leads to the question, what should the Church aspire to achieve as she reenters these contexts? Simply put, her sole goal should be to produce individuals who know Christ, live like Christ, and take Christ to the world. Christ must be central in all she does and all she pursues. From the beginning to the end, the centrality of Christ must be critical in every endeavor and must serve as the only mark of success in evangelism. In other words, in re-evangelism, the church is only successful when Christ's followers look like Christ.

One of the major benefits of having a clear vision is it begins to impact every other component of the journey. For example, imagine you want to go on a trip, so you go to the city and purchase a car. This would be great; surely a car can take you on a journey. However, what if you are living in the Caribbean and the destination of your journey is England? In that case, you would have wasted money purchasing a car because it is impossible to drive from Barbados to England.

However, if the destination was determined before purchasing the vehicle to get there, not only would money be saved, but the right means of transportation would be chosen. The principle is, the destination determines the vehicle, which in turn determines the journey. Insisting on the centrality of Christ in re-evangelism will begin to impact every other area of the Church's evangelistic effort.

One may wonder if this was not the vision from the very beginning. From a biblical perspective, yes. From an experiential perspective, no. In many cases, the issues that emerged in the countries oversaturated with the Gospel came about because the Church became satisfied with conversions alone instead of also leading new converts toward Christlikeness. Repeating the sinner's prayer became the measure of her success as opposed to bearing fruit of true repentance and becoming more like Christ. As a result, it is critical to reaffirm that the Church's primary role is to point others to Christ and to help them become like Him.

To be clear, such a vision should directly impact and transform our evangelism strategies. If our destination is to be like Christ and see others become like Him, immediately our vehicles must change. Now, we are not simply evangelizing for someone to repeat a prayer after us. We are evangelizing with the hope that, not only will the person be saved, but also set out on a journey of becoming like Christ. If we adopt this line of thinking, we will hardly ever view evangelism and discipleship as separate entities again.

Holistic Mission

A few years ago, a team of Nazarene missionaries embarked on a seven-month missional journey across the Mesoamerica Region. One of the participants of this trip had an encounter that took place while evangelizing in a community in a Caribbean island called St. Kitts. While in the field, they came across a man of the Rastafarian religion who was completely anti-church. His language and attitude clearly indicated that he had no interest in hearing anything the team had to say or to offer.

Interestingly, the team decided they were going to engage in a community service project and clean up the community they were evangelizing. To their surprise, the man who had no interest in what they had to offer joined them in the field, picking up garbage and cleaning the community. He eventually commented, "this is what the Church is for!", alluding to the fact that the church must have more to offer than words. As a result, the man became more open to what the team had to say and offer.

Jesus, and in turn the Scriptures, is a firm supporter of holistic mission. Holistic mission refers to the church's ability and intentionality to reach the holistic needs of the individuals and communities they serve. Throughout the Scriptures, Jesus is seen meeting spiritual, physical, and even emotional needs.

The reason why this approach is emphasized as an aspect of re-evangelism is due to a norm in countries overly saturated with the Gospel. Churches in these contexts are usually one-dimensional, primarily seeking to address the spiritual issues. As a matter of fact, many of the perceived damages the Church has caused have stemmed from a one-dimensional approach to ministry. Holistic mission is not only biblical, but it is a relevant and effective tool in re-evangelism.

I once had the opportunity to hear Dr. Ravi Jayakaran, senior associate for integral holistic mission in the Lausanne Movement, present on holistic mission. During this talk Dr. Jayakaran stated, "there are three clear components that must be a part of integral mission: words, works, and wonders." I personally want to add one more: whole life.

Words

Words refer to the fact that in holistic missions, the word of God must be verbally and audibly communicated. People must hear the true, undiluted Gospel in a language that they can understand. Without words, holistic mission is incomplete.

Works

Works refer to the acts of service that we as the Church must engage in within the communities we serve. Wherever we go, there will be needs. In some cases, the needs will be more obvious than others, but we can be sure that needs will be present. We as the Church, have the responsibility to respond to the needs of others. Just like the team in St. Kitts, we must put the love of God on display.

Wonders

Wonders refer to the supernatural involvement of God. In holistic mission, we are not only interested in the social and community needs, but we are also interested in the spiritual and health needs. Holistic mission provides a platform for God to perform healings and miracles in the lives of people around us. Wonders are a necessary component to holistic mission.

Whole Life

By whole life, I am referring to the fact that my life plays a critical role in mission. One of the major ways we can heal the damage that was once caused by the church is through the way we live. Whole life involves being individuals of integrity and truly representing what it means to be transformed by God.

Through engaging in these four elements, we are well on our way to being the salt and light of the world (Matthew 5:13-16). Through holistic mission, we let our light so shine, that men may see our good works and glorify our Father in heaven (Matthew 5:16).

Prayer

History is filled with numerous occasions when humans witnessed tremendous moves of God. One thing these moves of God have in common is the fact that the Church was praying.

For many, prayer is simply defined as a conversation between us and God. However, the Scriptures portray prayer as more than a conversation. It is also communicated as a vehicle. It is how we invite God into our issues for the primary goal of seeing His Kingdom come and His will done in the midst of our crises. If there is one place God is extremely needed, it is in our evangelistic efforts.

We must remember that evangelism, whether in a context that is oversaturated with the Gospel or in one where the Gospel has never been preached, is first and foremost a spiritual issue. Though the deception, desensitization, and damage caused by the popular Gospel can serve as hindrances as mentioned before, at the very root of it will always be a spiritual issue called sin. Hence, spiritual issues demand spiritual solutions. The only real and effective solution there is to the spiritual issue of sin is Jesus Christ.

This is why prayer is an imperative part of our efforts. Through prayer, we acknowledge the true issue and extend an invitation to the True Solution to come and resolve the issues we are facing. Through prayer, we are acknowledging that no matter the context, we in ourselves have no power to save anyone; the only one who is able to save is Jesus Christ. Prayer invites Jesus to liberate men and women from sin, bring truth where they are deceived, conviction where they have been desensitized, and healing where they have been damaged.

There is also another dimension where prayer is critical to re-evangelism. On one hand, prayer is important for the transformation of the people we are trying to reach as discussed before; on the other hand, prayer is also important for the transformation of our hearts and our posture towards the people we desire to reach. There are two things that are always important in any form of evangelism: our perception of the people we desire to reach and the posture of our heart toward them.

We must remember that evangelism, whether in a context that is oversaturated with the gospel, or in one where the gospel has never been preached, is first and foremost a spiritual issue.

Matthew 9:35-38 serves as an excellent illustration to this point. These few verses give a glimpse into Jesus' ministry. Matthew 9:36 says that Jesus was in the process of preaching and healing throughout the land: "When he saw the crowds, he had compassion on them, because they were harassed and helpless, like sheep without a shepherd." This one verse portrays both Jesus' perception of the people (they were harassed and helpless, like sheep without a shepherd) and the posture of His heart toward them (he had compassion on them).

It must be noted that it was how Jesus perceived them that defined the posture of His heart. He had compassion because He did not see them as nuisances or as worthless. Jesus saw people who were harassed and helpless, in need of guidance. This perception drove Him to compassion, which in turn inspired Him to positive action to see these people relieved.

Similarly, we must be the same. We must have the right perception and the right posture toward the people we serve. In a context that is oversaturated with the Gospel, this can be difficult sometimes. It is easy to start viewing people as hopeless and beyond God's reach, especially in a context where they are familiar with the Gospel and consistently refuse to receive it. This can make us bitter and judgmental, which in turn affects our effectiveness.

Prayer is one major strategy that keeps our perspective and posture in the right place. As we pray for people, the Holy Spirit is able to soften our hearts and keep us patient and compassionate toward the people we serve. Re-evangelism will be a tedious process, and if we are to achieve it our hearts must be in the right place.

Clearly, the role of prayer in re-evangelism is important. It is necessary for both our hearts and the hearts of those we intend to reach. Church history is filled with examples of the power of prayer to see transformation in any context, and the nations where there is an oversaturation of the Gospel are no different. Through prayer, we can witness a significant move of God in our context.

Re-evangelizing nations which are oversaturated with the Gospel will not be an easy task, however, it is possible. As we become aware of the issues that currently exist within these contexts — deception, desensitization, and damage — and make a decision to be a part of God's solution to these issues, we can experience the change we long to see. As we put Christ first, adopt a posture of prayer, and engage in holistic mission, we can experience the change we long for.

WORKS CITED/NOTES

Introduction

1. Oden, Thomas C. *John Wesley's Teachings, Volume 2: Christ and Salvation* [Kindle Edition]. Zondervan, 2012.

    This work of the Spirit is the form of grace that Wesley called "going before grace," or "prevenient grace." The Latin root makes this clearer. Prevenient grace is treated as an article of faith in the Articles of Religion. Prevenient grace is moving the sinner toward the fullness of grace even before its saving implications are recognized.

2. Kipp, Mike, Kenny Wade. *Being Real: Sharing Your Faith without Losing Your Friends*. Barefoot Ministries of Kansas City, 2007.

Chapter 1

1. Schmelzenbach, Harmon Faldine. *Schmelzenbach of Africa: The Story of Harmon F. Schmelzenbach, Missionary Pioneer to Swaziland, South Africa*. Nazarene Publishing House, 1971.

2. Barrs, Jerram. *Learning Evangelism from Jesus*. Crossway, 2009.

3. Ibid.

4. Bustle, Louie E., Stan Toler. *Each One Win One*. Beacon Hill Press of Kansas City, 2006.

Chapter 2

1. Platt, David. *Follow Me: A Call to Die. A Call to Live*. Tyndale House Publishers, Inc., 2013.

2. Chambers, Oswald. *My Utmost for His Highest: 2016 Grad Edition*. Barbour Books, 2016.

Chapter 4

1. Smith, Oswald J. *El avivamiento que necesitamos*. Xulon Press, 1925.

2. Stott, John. *A Missão Cristã no Mundo Moderno*. Falcon, 1975.

3. "Vulnerabilidade social." *Wikipedia.org*, pt.wikipedia.org/wiki/Vulnerabilidade_social. 7 May 2017.

Chapter 6

1. Thorsen, Don. *An Exploration of Christian Theology*. Baker Academic, 2008.

2. "Postcristianismo." *Wikipedia.org*, es.wikipedia.org/wiki/Poscristianismo. 24 April 2017.

3. Jones, E. Stanley. *Mahatma Gandhi: An Interpretation*. Lucknow Pub. House, 1991.

4. Ibid.

www.ingramcontent.com/pod-product-compliance
Lightning Source LLC
Chambersburg PA
CBHW021143020426
42331CB00005B/873